X 3⁵³⁵ ᵉᵗ
ᵐⁱⁿᵈ

WITHDRAWN
UTSA LIBRARIES

Restoration
TRAGEDY
1660–1720

Oxford University Press, Ely House, London W. 1

GLASGOW NEW YORK TORONTO MELBOURNE WELLINGTON
CAPE TOWN SALISBURY IBADAN NAIROBI LUSAKA ADDIS ABABA
BOMBAY CALCUTTA MADRAS KARACHI LAHORE DACCA
KUALA LUMPUR HONG KONG

FIRST EDITION 1929
REPRINTED LITHOGRAPHICALLY IN GREAT BRITAIN
AT THE UNIVERSITY PRESS, OXFORD
FROM SHEETS OF THE FIRST EDITION
1950 (CORRECTED), 1954, 1959 (CORRECTED)
1963, 1966

*R*estoration
T R A G E D Y
1660 – 1720

BY

BONAMY DOBRÉE

OXFORD

At the Clarendon Press

Study is only a serious form of gossip

E. M. FORSTER

To

T. S. ELIOT

PREFACE

It was the writing of the chapter Cleopatra and 'that Criticall Warr' as a separate study which stimulated my curiosity, beyond that of the ordinary cursory reader of Restoration tragedy, to the making of this book. That chapter appeared in a shorter form in The Times Literary Supplement. I was further spurred on by an invitation to write an article on Otway in the same paper when the Nonesuch edition of Otway's works was published. An article on Dryden was also printed in the same place. Though these chapters have undergone a certain amount of expansion and alteration to fit them into the scheme of this book I wish to thank the editor of the Literary Supplement both for the hospitality of his columns and for permission to reprint the articles here.

My thanks are also due, indeed long overdue, to the Delegates of the Clarendon Press and their staff for their unfailing patience and courtesy; and not only for their encouragement, but also for the ready assistance they have given me on several occasions.

I should also state that some of the material scattered about the book has appeared in different form in the Introduction to the World's Classics edition of Five Restoration Tragedies.

B.D.

October 1929.

CONTENTS

INTRODUCTION

If it be true that all art is an exploration of life, just as philosophy and science are so in their diverse ways, then it should be possible to distinguish between the various forms of art by mapping out the regions they attempt. Precision is not to be hoped for, since overlapping is at once obvious, and the geographer must of necessity be allowed vagueness at the edges. In literature we may, for instance, try to define the lyric as the form in which man explores his impulses, and often his revolt ; the epic, that where he investigates his sense of adventure, physical or spiritual ; comedy, that where he inquires into himself as a social animal : but each realm would stake out its boundaries well within the neighbouring country. Keeping such latitude in mind, tragedy, which perhaps has a wider span than any other form, might be described as the realm where man explores his daring against the overwhelming odds of life, and tests the depth of his acceptance. It is somewhere here that the power of tragedy must be sought, with pity and fear as the means, not the end, as the accidents of the countryside, not the country itself. Tragedy, we may say, is man's trial of his individual strength, a trial becoming increasingly unpopular, indeed incomprehensible, with the advance of democracy.

One result immediately flows from this ; or perhaps it would be wiser to say that one observed fact, which can readily be put to the proof by any one, comes to the support of this doctrine. It is that tragedy, from the spectator's point of view, is the most personal of the literary forms. We identify ourselves with the persons of a tragedy as we watch it ; we are Orestes, or Macbeth, or John Gabriel

Borkmann; but we are not Philocleon, or Tartufe, or Lady Wishfort, whatever the moralists may say. In this connexion we can note Shakespeare's amazing capacity for making his people seem to act a part in life before themselves, and to this faculty may well be due some of his success as a writer of tragedy; for by his making his personages seem to act, the spectators more easily live the actors' parts. This, in its turn, if we allow ourselves to be tempted still further into this theory, explains why it is that the tragedy of an age always seems to be the surest indication of its temper, so far as such can be said to exist. Every real work of art is, of course, unique; but it is constructed out of the intuitions of the artist, which are in turn the product of the knowledge and outlook on life he cannot help sharing with his fellows. That is why, even if we probe far below the mere fashions of the day, the tragedies of a period are found closely to resemble one another; why we can speak with fairly accurate definition of Greek tragedy, or of Shakespearian tragedy; and why that of the Restoration differs from any that has been written at any time in England or any other country.

The tragedy of this period has, beyond denial, some relation to the French tragedy of the time, but it would seem that French influence has been as much exaggerated here as it used to be in the case of comedy. To trace influences is always an amusement yielding dubious results, and in any case influence is a seed that will only grow in soil already prepared for it. What probably occurs is this. One country is poking about for a certain thing which another country has already largely found; when the first country catches sight of this find, it hails it with joy as the very thing it has been wanting, and leaps over the normal intermediate stages. As regards Restoration tragedy, the classical formal element was already there with Ben Jonson : the heroic aspects were adumbrated, often in Fletcher and Massinger, and even in Shakespeare. Coriolanus is a figure of heroic tragedy, and so, indeed, is Tamburlaine. Viola is a 'heroic' woman, and no less so Fletcher's Evadne, or Ford's Annabella and Bianca. Mr. Eliot goes so far as to say, when speaking of Massinger, that ' The tendency of the romantic drama was towards a form which continued it in removing its more conspicuous vices, was towards a more severe external order. This form was the heroic drama.' The heroic aspects were, in the main, subdued in the great Shakespearian era, but they were seeking for outlet, for maturity. The mature state was at once seen to exist in Corneille, and this drove the Caroline writers to study him. But French plants do not easily bear a transfer into English earth; they are changed to such an extent that the most obvious things about them are their wholly English colourings when they are successful, and their absurdity, as of shams, when they fail.

Thus the object of these studies is threefold. The first is to see why Restoration tragedy took the form known as ' heroic ', and what the word implies; the second to distinguish the characteristics of some of the greater writers of the period, to see what were the objects they actually created; and lastly, since the study of the past is only of value as it affects the present, to see what lessons can be learnt for the writing of tragedy at the present day, though a less propitious age than ours could hardly be imagined. For tragedy, to reach a successful issue, must more than any other art (since it appeals immediately to the mass) be based either on some common metaphysic, or on some general impulse, and both these are notoriously lacking at the present time.

This book, then, does not pretend to be a complete study of the subject, nor an historical summing up, providing neat labels for tabulating ; it attempts rather to define a type and trace its development. If this is not enough to excuse the absence of Banks, Crowne, and Settle, it must be pleaded that there is a level below which it is waste of time for the mere lover of literature, as opposed to the scholar or thesis-writer, to go ; and indeed, grubbing in the mud in the hopes of making mud look like crystal, or of finding some isolated, and even then doubtful, gem in the slime, is much to be deplored. Yet, in spite of its gaps, it is hoped that this volume may have its interest for those who are attracted by the critical problems of literature, especially of the drama, as well as for those who are interested in the period itself, and find its transient freaks as important and illuminating as its enduring beauties.

I

THE NECESSITY FOR HEROISM

Le donne, i cavalier, l'armi, gli amori,
le cortesie, l'audaci' imprese io canto.

Ariosto.

Social Reasons.

THE aspect which first strikes every reader of Restoration tragedy is its unreality—not of plot or of homely detail, for all tragedy worthy of the name from the plays of Aeschylus to *Faust* is unreal with respect to fact—but in the flagrant unreality of the emotions involved. The test of truth in a tragedy is to be applied not to the facts, but to the feelings. We ask ourselves whether, placed in the situations of the people portrayed, and making allowance for their beliefs, would we, or anybody we know, feel and behave as they do? The acknowledged tragedies of the world stand the test well enough, and no one bothers his head about verisimilitude. But how, in heaven's name, we say, did a whole generation come to accept the fantastic ideas of valour, the absurd notions of dauntless, unquenchable love, we find in Restoration tragedy? These things simply do not correspond with experience. We are at once aware that this tragedy is written on another theory to that we are sensible of in Sophocles, Shakespeare, or Racine, made of different materials. It is all 'heroic', whether written in rhymed couplets or not. How then did the playwrights of that age come to write as they did? To us it seems at first incomprehensible, but to the men of those days the answer was quite plain, and was expressed for them by Hobbes: 'the work of an heroic poem is to raise admiration, principally for three virtues, valour, beauty, and love'. No phrase could more neatly provide criticism with the instruments proper to the occasion.

For when, in 1700, Addison wrote of Boileau to Bishop Hough: ' Aristotle, says he, proposes two passions that are proper to be raised by tragedy, terror and pity, but Corneille endeavours at a new one, which is admiration', he might have added that to endeavour at admiration had been the hallmark of all English tragedy for the last forty odd years. Corneille, in his own opinion, was only using what means he could to arouse fear and pity, but though he based himself on Aristotle, he admitted that he diverged from the practice of the ancients in making his heroes lovable, in contradistinction with Orestes or Electra, whom he did not like at all: ' ainsi notre maxime de faire aimer les principaux acteurs n'étoit pas de l'usage des anciens ' he explained in his *Second Discours*. And then, some pages further on, we see what occurs in attempting to distort life: ' le but du poète est de plaire selon les règles de son art: pour plaire, il a besoin quelquefois de rehausser l'éclat des belles actions et d'exténuer l'horreur des funestes '. That much admitted, the floodgates of admiration can no longer be kept closed, provided, of course, that that is the sort of thing the audience wants.

It would be over-cautious not to say outright that the post-Restoration audience did want it, firstly for social reasons, secondly for aesthetic, though in making the distinction their common origin in the desires of man must not be lost sight of. As regards social reasons, England was then passing through a period of disillusion after a cycle of actions which ought to have been glorious enough, but which the event proved disappointing. Few ideals can stand the test of actuality, and there seemed to be a gap between what, to those who had read history, ought to have been

magnificently glorious, and the humdrumness of the events
in real life. Hampden, no doubt, was well enough, but was
he to be compared with Brutus? Did the thought of Crom-
well, even in the hearts of his partisans, evoke quite the
same emotions as the idea of Cæsar? It was odd, but if you
met General Monck at dinner, you did not feel that you
had, as it were, been hobnobbing with Catiline. It was easy
to label pretenders, but even the adulatory labels you glued
on in all honesty seemed to have a certain irony about them.
Those whom you hailed as historic figures in the glow of
a genial evening appeared strangely shrunk when you met
them walking in the Mall the next day, or cheapening a pair
of gloves at the New Exchange.

> Go seek the novice statesmen, and obtrude
> On them some Roman cast similitude,
> Tell them of liberty, the stories fine,
> Until you all grow consuls in your wine :
> Or thou, *Dictator* of the glass, bestow
> On him the *Cato*, this the *Cicero*.

So Marvell wrote in *Tom May's Death*; and Otway echoed
the jibe in *Venice Preserv'd*, when the sorry conspirators
meet together (II. iii):

Pierre.	Friends! was not Brutus,
	(I mean that Brutus, who in open senate
	Stabbed the first Cæsar that usurped the world)
	A gallant man?
Renault.	Yes, and Catiline too ;
	Tho' story wrong his fame : for he conspired
	To prop the reeling glory of his country :
	His cause was good.
Bedamar.	And ours as much above it,
	As Renault thou'rt superior to Cethegus,
	Or Pierre to Cassius.

And later (IV. ii), Belvidera asks,

> Where's now the Roman constancy I boasted?

as though it were quite naturally to Rome that anybody would turn for comparisons. The reality of an apparently indecisive civil war seemed lamentably unepic when weighed in the balance with a Roman *coup d'état*.

Literary Influence.

The age, then, was hungry for heroism, and feeling itself baulked of it in real life was happy to find it in its art. What was art for but to provide what was lacking in everyday existence? Something in life had been missed which it might be precisely the function of art to purvey. To-day, such a statement of the function of art is sufficiently scoffed at as the aesthetic doctrine of the servant girl who greedily devours novels where the Duke marries the tweeny. Yet it may well be questioned whether such doctrine does not lurk at the base of a good deal of aesthetic criticism at the present, or any day, especially where 'sublimity' is demanded, as though the poet were not to concern himself with common things.*
In the middle of the seventeenth century no one was shy of making such a claim for art, and had for authority no less a person than Bacon, whose views pervaded the whole century. The aim and object of poetry, he wrote, ' is to give some shadow of satisfaction to the mind of man in those points

* Thus Professor Whitehead, in *Science and the Modern World* (Chap. XIII) : ' Great art is the arrangement of the environment, so as to provide for the soul vivid, but transient values. Human beings require something which absorbs them for a time, something out of the routine which they can stare at'; and Mr. F. L. Lucas, in *Tragedy* (p. 52) : ' And so we go to tragedies not in the least to get rid of emotions, but to have them more abundantly ; to banquet, not to purge. Our lives are often dull, they are always brief in duration and confined in scope ; but here, vicariously, the being " whose dull morrow cometh and is as to-day is " can experience something more.'

where the nature of things doth deny it . . . by substituting
the shows of things to the desires of the mind'. Man,
dissatisfied with the prosaic nature of things as they are,
uses the imagination to shadow forth the poetry of things as
they should be.

Here Corneille and Bacon are at one : Macbeth is as un-
lovable as Orestes, therefore the tragedies that deal with
them are peccant works of art. And this psychological
criticism derived support from purely literary criticism,
which went back to Aristotle for authority, especially to
that part of the *Poetics* where it is stated that 'tragedy is
an imitation of personages better than the ordinary man ',
who should be made handsomer than he is. It was again
Hobbes who made the point quite clearly : ' the delight of
an Epic Poem consisteth not in mirth, but in admiration ',
he wrote in his answer to Davenant (1650), ten years before
Corneille's essay was published, where he maintained also
that ' the figure . . . of an Epic Poem and of a Tragedy ought
to be the same '. Here he was really agreeing with Davenant, who was of the opinion that ' to make great actions
credible is the principal art of poets '. It is curious that
even Dryden, for all his admiration of Ben Jonson, should
have fallen into the same error : ' These heroic representations are of the same nature as the epic', he stated,
although the author of *Discoveries* had noted that ' the
space of the action may not prove large enough for the
epic fable, yet may be perfect for the dramatic, and whole ',
implying that the scope of the drama was not to be so
catholic as that of the epic.

Such, in the main, was the outlook, and on the point
where these two approaches met there also converged the
way of humanistic criticism, which throughout the century,
from Ben Jonson onward (though with occasional dissenti-

ents), declared loudly that the business of art was to in-
struct as well as to please. The century did not lack its
Ruskins to declare that art was the handmaiden of morality; but the didactic method was not so much that of
portraying the sad results of evil actions, as was the way
of Bunyan in *The Life and Death of Mr. Badman*, of Hogarth
in *The Idle Apprentice*, and, on the whole, of the nineteenth
century, as that of producing striking examples fit not
only for general imitation, but especially for the imitation
of the great. Thus Davenant wrote in his preface to *Gondibert* :

> Princes and nobles, being reformed and made angelical by
> the heroic, will be predominant lights, which the people can-
> not choose but use for direction, as glowworms take in and keep
> the sun's beams till they shine and make day to themselves.

It is doubtful, however, if Davenant really believed in
this process of extracting sunbeams out of cucumbers, for
he definitely stated another principle, which chimed in
well with Aristotle, namely the aristocratic principle of
art being for the high, and not for the mob. ' The common
crowd, of whom we are hopeless, we desert ', both as fit
to be made into examples, and fitted to judge of them.
The touchstone of common feeling was evidently to be
abandoned, and, after all, Restoration tragedy was prim-
arily a courtly art, written for the King's Players, or the
Duke of York's Players, to act before fashionable audiences,
and not meant for the groundlings of the Phœnix or
the Globe. It would be easy to make too much of this
attitude in determining why this tragedy took the form it
did, for human activities rarely have a single cause; it is
rather a mass of small things bearing on one point which
brings about anything decisive, or even worthy of note.
At the same time, this view must have had some force,

for if it was the duty of art to profit as well as to delight, it was obviously no use trying to teach virtues to such ordinary mortals as would not be able to put them into practice.

Such imitation of high things served yet a further purpose; the stage might almost claim to remedy, or supply, the failings of the church, which the 'laziness or dullness' of priests had allowed to desert rhyme, although the uses of poetry were not to be compared with those of divinity. Still,

> By the harmony of words we elevate the mind to a sense of devotion, as our solemn music, which is inarticulate poesy, does in churches. And by the lively images of piety, adorned by action, through the senses allure the soul: which while it is charmed in a silent joy of what it sees and hears, is struck at the same time with a secret veneration of things celestial, and is wound up insensibly into the practice of that which it admires.

So Dryden in the preface to *Tyrannick Love*; but alas! though we can rise to great occasions, and can be virtuous enough if we feel that enough depends upon our virtue, most of us do not have to beware of becoming prigs however many elevating plays we may see.

The Effects of Admiration.

Admiration, then, aided by the harmony of words, took the place of terror in these dramas, as might also be deduced from the number of happy endings. But terror is made impure by admiration, and where the latter rules, pity cannot hold its own. If one side of the balance is altered, some compensation must be made on the other; and this came to be provided, naturally enough, by an especial treatment of love. The work of an heroic poem is to raise admiration, principally for three virtues, valour, beauty, and love. None but the brave deserves the fair, and naturally, the more wonderfully brave the hero, the more virtuously fair must the heroine be. It would seem to follow almost logically. But the reason why love fell in so pat with the needs of the audience was partly ethical, and partly social. It was ethical in so far that in ages of growing scepticism, and during this period if you were not a professed Hobbist you could at least fling a jeer at Muggleton, love attains inordinate importance. When men cannot be certain of their souls they are the readier prey of their emotions, for when there is no external authority for men to rely on, they turn in upon themselves. Socially, the same causes were at work as in the matter of heroic bravery; art provided what life denied. The average moral life of the courtiers is too notorious to need re-statement: Whitehall the naked Venus first revealed, and though the state of affairs might have its excitements, it also had its discomforts. The love motive might have gained support from a misunderstanding of Racine, but it was a natural growth in a society which could find in its art, as opposed to life, nothing more admirable than heroic constancy and faultlessly noble sentiments.

It is, however, not merely that perfect love was exhibited for admiration, but that it was used as the means for procuring pity: indeed, it is hardly going too far to say that the misfortunes of love alone were relied upon to gain this end. Heroic failure, heroic death—and often heroic success—are so admirable and desirable in themselves, that they call for no pity. Who would not be an immortal hero at the price of a momentary death-pang? The fallen fortunes of the great were paid lip service, but they were not given tragic force. Passionate love, then, became a necessary part of tragedy. It had not been necessary in Shakespeare; it is quite absent from some of his greatest works, though he could use it when he wished as a main element, as in *Romeo and Juliet*, and in *Antony and Cleopatra*. The ingredients of Restoration work were, in short, not terror and pity, but terror-admiration with love-pity.

Nor was the love quite of the normal kind, a legacy perhaps from the 'Platonic love' of the Court of Henrietta Maria: not only was it virtuous beyond the wildest dreams, but all other virtues had to give way before it. A sound, guaranteed heroic love was excuse for any betrayal of friendship or dereliction of duty. It was a law unto itself that overbore all other laws. Thus Cortez says in *The Indian Emperor*:

> Honour begone, what art thou, but a breath?
> I'll live, proud of my infamy and shame,
> Graced with no triumph but a lover's name;
> Men can but say, love did his reason blind,
> And love's the noblest frailty of the mind.

Later romantic poets never went so far in making duty to love the pre-eminent duty, but in the heroic world it was almost shameful not to betray your country if love demanded it of you, so that, though the errors of love were called upon to catch votes for pity, the voting cards dropped into the box were often counted for admiration. Man's failure to control his pride or his passion, a proper subject for tragedy, was deftly turned to account in merely dazzling the imagination. Such transcending love might well sweep before it all other considerations:

> Ev'n Jove would try more shapes her love to win:
> And in new birds, and unknown beasts would sin;
> At least, if Jove could love like Maximin.

(*Tyrannick Love*, II.)

Thus, in this tragedy we find man, not so much exploring his daring and measuring his acceptance, as reaching for the absolute, trying to establish something definite in opposition to the unsatisfactory compromises of life. It is the reverse of most of the comedy of the period, which on the whole very much accepted the human animal for what he was, however much it may have declared its wish to profit. It is true that something of the same quality, the search for the absolute, is to be found in Wycherley; but it is normal for comedy to seek the average, and the comedy of that period did so very consistently in the main. Tragedy, for a variety of causes, attempted to cure humanity of itself by presenting the exalted picture.

The Influence of the Theatre.

It was aided in this, spurred on even, by the development of the stage itself; and for the first time, perhaps, were felt the vicious effects of allowing boards and bricks and mortar to dictate to literature, though influence it to a certain extent they must. With the more complicated scenery something of the masque element entered into tragedy, not as a literary form but as a spectacle. The eye as well as the mind had to be staggered: or perhaps, since the eye was astounded, the words had to beat the scenery at its own game. 'Our theatres now,' Richard Flecknoe wrote (1664),

> for cost and ornament are arrived to the height of magnificence; but that which makes our stage the better makes our plays the worse perhaps, they striving now to make them more for sight than hearing, whence that solid joy of the interior is lost, and that benefit which men formerly received from plays, from which they seldom or never went away but far better and wiser than they came.

Davenant gave the lead in his theatre, with his experiments in stage-craft; and the Duke's theatre, finding it draw the public, was forced to follow suit. What did words matter, when you had the gorgeous painted scene, with all sorts of amusing contraptions? 'Now, gentlemen,' Bayes remarks at the beginning of the last act of *The Rehearsal*, ' I will be bold to say, I'll show you the greatest scene that England ever saw: I mean not for words, for those I do not value; but for state, show, and magnificence.' Moreover, as when '*the two right Kings of* Brentford *descend in the Clouds*' our attention is still more clearly directed to the effect the masque had, especially in its machines, which make such pleasant reading when described by Ben Jonson, and which gave Inigo Jones fine scope for his ingenious art. ' Representations by the Art of Perspective ' such as Davenant adopted for *The Siege of Rhodes* were probably child's play to the carpentry that could compose for Lee's *Sophonisba* ' *a Heaven of Blood, two Suns, Spirits in Battle, Arrows shot to and fro in the Air.*' The most extravagant development was naturally in the operatic pieces, which show to what lengths this sort of amusement could be carried, and the sort of thing the audiences were likely to appreciate in more purely literary work. For Dryden's *The State of Innocence* we have '*A sun gloriously rising and moving orbicularly; at a distance, below, is the Moon; the part next the Sun enlightened, the other dark. A black Cloud comes whirling from the adverse part of the Heavens bearing Lucifer in it; at his nearer approach the Body of the Sun is darkened.*' Then, after a speech of Lucifer's, '*From that Part of the Heavens where the Sun appears, a Chariot is discover'd drawn with White Horses, and in it* Uriel *the Regent of the Sun. The chariot moves swiftly towards* Lucifer, *and at* Uriel's *Approach the Sun recovers his height.*' In *Albion and Albianus*, Juno appears in a machine drawn by peacocks, which ' *opens and discovers the Tail of the Peacock, which is so large that it almost fills the opening of the Stage between Scene and Scene.*' ' As the width of the Dorset Garden stage was about thirty feet,' Professor Nicoll comments, ' this indi-

cates an extent of well over twenty feet for the peacock's tail.'
Nor was noise absent, for we read in *The Censure of the
Rota*, 'An heroic poem never sounded so nobly, as when it
was heightened with shouts and clashing of swords; . . .
drums and trumpets gained an absolute dominion over the
mind of the audience.'

With a background of that sort, what could the author
do but invest his characters with the most extravagant sentiments, make them rant and fume in the most bombastic
manner ? No wonder that muscle became an important part
of the hero's make-up! Amid such competitors what less
could Drawcansir say than

> Others may boast a single man to kill;
> But I, the blood of thousands, daily spill.
> Let petty Kings the names of Parties know :
> Where e'er I come, I slay both friend and foe.
> (*The Rehearsal*, v.)

What less could little Maximins do than defy the gods ?
Yet, easy as it was, and is, to ridicule Restoration tragedy,
it was popular : it corresponded with certain definite needs
in the minds and emotions of men. It has virtues and
charms ; in its setting it may even have appeared plausible;
it was 'not the business of a poet to represent historical
truth, but probability ', as Dryden remarked in the Epistle
Dedicatory of *The Conquest of Mexico*. Besides, it mapped
out a range of human feeling in a manner which it will, in
later chapters, be our business to consider, not as a necessary
product of its age, but as a method which did produce objects
worth looking at.

II

RESTORATION CRITICISM; AND THE TREND OF WRITING

The Precepts: Romanticism.

ANOTHER of the many reasons which make interesting the study of Restoration drama, is that it was the literary centre of those days. The point of battle had shifted from poetry to plays; and instead of *The Arte of Poesie* or a *Defence of Rime*, we get the *Essay of Dramatick Poesy* as the type of writing, though, naturally, discursions on pure poetry were not lacking. For in poetry, one side, the side of smoothness, had, thanks to Waller, definitely gained the victory for the age—at least as far as critics were concerned. But now for the first time arose active discussion of plays; not that it had been altogether absent before, witness Sidney and Ben Jonson, but it had not been general. Now, from Davenant's *Preface to Gondibert* (1650) to beyond the Collier controversy at the end of the century, literary excitement rose higher about stage writing than about any other kind. Critics multiplied, for no one was afraid to tackle what everybody enjoyed: and it is certain that Restoration tragedy cannot be properly understood without taking note of the critical ideas of the day.

The main battle of the writers themselves was on the point of form, the 'classical' as against the 'modern' Unluckily, the question was treated neither abstractly, as we should do nowadays, with one eye on psychology, nor from the point of view of content. It was almost always a matter of authority, or at any rate of precedents. It never

occurred to the critics that content and form were inter-
dependent; that a definite mould, suitable for obtaining
certain results, or for expressing a well-defined attitude,
might not be so well fitted for other purposes. Had they
considered such a relation, and had the word romantic
been familiar, and treated, as has since been the usage, as
antithetical to classical, they might have been aware of an
entertaining state of things. As it is, we are provided with
a clue as to why the tragedy of the period failed to please
except for a short time : the reason is that the dramatists of
that day were trying to express romantic ideas in a form
specially evolved for the classical.

So much dust has been raised about these two words, as
is inevitable when words are used as whips to beat the
very dust with, that it may be as well to define the sense
in which they are used in this place. As regards the
form of plays, the word classical is reserved for the style
which served Ben Jonson and Racine ; that is, one with
close attention paid to the three unities as regarded by
Renaissance writers to be what Aristotle taught, or at
least implied. The romantic is anything else ; but to
avoid confusion of words, the name 'panoramic' will
be given to the Shakespearian form. As regards matter,
the following distinctions will be maintained, without
prejudice as to respective values. The romantic writer
is one who will not, or cannot, accept the limitations
of existence : he is for 'the light that never was on sea
or land'; he is for the individual defying the Universe;
he is Prometheus or Rimbaud. Incidentally, of course, he
shatters convention. The classical writer, on the other
hand, definitely does accept human limitations : he is con-
scious of a humane tradition ; he finds the life he knows
rich enough fare for him, and is not urged to go outside it.

For him, life is a material with definite characteristics, which can be dealt with, no doubt, in various ways, but which cannot be greatly altered. The romantic is always in revolt, eager to remould the world nearer *his* heart's desire: the value of his work, therefore, depends not upon experience, whether personal or the accumulated experience of mankind, but upon the quality of his heart. Shelley, therefore, is a good romantic, and Byron is not. And what is curious about Restoration tragedy is, that however much it may conform to classical order, the passions expressed in it are nearly always the romantic passions: in it the limitations of human nature, one might almost say of nature, are disregarded, and even flouted.

It was deliberate: again and again we find it stated that the business of the poet is to make the impossible appear likely. The improbable was a trifling matter. Sir Robert Howard, for instance, declared that ' it is not necessary for poets to study strict reason, since they are so used to a greater latitude than is allowed by that severe inquisition '. Dryden again, in *An Essay on Heroick Plays* (the Preface to *The Conquest of Granada*), remarked that :

> If any man object the improbabilities of a spirit appearing, or of a raised palace by magic; I boldly answer him, that an heroic poet is not tied to a bare representation of what is true, or exceeding probable; but that he might let himself loose to visionary objects, and to the representation of such things, as depending not on sense, and therefore not to be comprehended by knowledge, may give him a freer scope for imagination.

This was to go somewhat beyond the letter of the law, as laid down by Ben Jonson, though it started from the same point. In *Discoveries* Dryden may have read that the poet took his name ' from the word ποιεῖν, which signifies to make or feign. Hence he is called a poet, not he which writeth in measure only, but that feigneth and formeth a fable, and writes things like the truth'. Like the truth—there's the rub. Jonson, who was classical in every sense of the word, stuck close to experience, however imaginatively he may have portrayed it. Restoration truth was that of the ideal: its heroes were not men as they are, but men as the writers would have liked them to be. That we would not like them to be so is neither here nor there. The Restoration dramatists moulded men nearer to their hearts' desire, circumstances having made them desire men like that. It was the duty of the imagination to supply the gaps in nature. So Dryden quoted from Petronius:

> Non enim res gestæ versibus comprehendendæ sunt ; quod longè melius Historici faciunt : sed, per ambages, Deorumque ministeria, [ ] præcipitandus est liber Spiritus, ut potius furentis animi vaticinatio appareat, quam religiosæ orationis, sub testibus, fides.*

Granting the romantic basis of Restoration work, it is not surprising to find in *Biographia Literaria* : ' *Praecipitandus est liber spiritus*, says Petronius most happily. The epithet, *liber*, here balances the preceding verb; and it is not easy to conceive more meaning condensed in fewer words.' It is doubtful if Coleridge found himself much akin to the Restoration writers, but they would probably have found much in him with which they could heartily agree. For them beauty was truth, if it could be made to appear plausible; that the truth was not beauty is merely another

---

* ' It is not a question of recording real events in verse ; historians can do that far better. The free spirit of genius must plunge headlong into allusions and divine interpositions, so that what results seems rather the prophecies of an inspired seer than the exactitude of a statement made on oath before witnesses.' Loeb Classics: *The Satyricon*, partially translated by M. Heseltine.

indication that the temper of their minds was not classical. The basis of Restoration tragedy is the Romantic idea.

Common Sense.

The common-sense reaction did not fail to make its appearance. Its great champion was Thomas Rymer, though *The Rehearsal* made an earlier protest than his, and one that was vigorous enough. But Rymer went too far: he did not realize that given the state of excitement the drama can induce in us (never mind the means), we can accept things which in our calmer moments we would reject as absurd, and that a play must be judged drunk as well as sober. Or rather, if he realized it, he would not admit it. ' But if neither the show nor the action cheats us, there remains still a notable vehicle to carry off nonsense, which is the pronunciation.' And he capped his statement with a quotation from Waller:

> By the loud trumpet which our courage aids,
> We learn, that sound as well as sense persuades.

But the point lies in whether or not we can be persuaded, or, if you will, cheated. It was not so much upon likeness to life that he insisted, as on decorum, and he was the forerunner of Dennis in the stress he laid upon correctness. His famous remark that ' Poetical decency will not suffer death to be dealt to each other by such persons whom the laws of duels allow not to enter the lists together', is enough to prove that for him poetical decency had nothing to do with everyday actuality. The whole question is really one of limits, and these he defined accurately enough.

Though the poet must have large knowledge, he ' must have judgement to select what is noble or beautiful, and proper for his occasion. He must by a particular chemistry extract the essence of things, without soiling his wit with the gross and trumpery', he remarked in the *Preface to Rapin* (1674). The question naturally arises, what, in this connection, is trumpery? Well, common feeling must decide. Thus, in *The Tragedies of the Last Age* (1678):

> Say others, poetry and reason, how come these to be cater-cousins? Poetry is the child of fancy, and is never to be schooled and disciplined by reason; poetry, say they, is blind inspiration, is pure enthusiasm, is rapture and rage all over.
>
> But fancy, I think, in poetry, is like faith in religion: it makes far discoveries, and soars above reason, but never clashes or runs against it. Fancy leaps and frisks, and away she's gone, whilst reason rattles the chains and follows after. Reason must consent and ratify whatever by fancy is attempted in its absence, or else 'tis all null and void in law. However, in the contrivance and economy of a play, reason is always principally to be consulted. Those who object against reason are fanatics in poetry, and are never to be saved by their good works.

Sense, that was really the main contention: 'We want a law for acting *The Rehearsal* once a week, to keep us in our sense.'

Rymer's most important contribution, however, was the application of the notion of 'poetical justice', (a term which, according to Dr. Spingarn, he invented), and in which he was followed by Dennis and Dr. Johnson, not to stretch as far as Ruskin. Dryden took the phrase up for only a short time in his criticism, but he often applied the notion in practice, and it was evidently in the air. Indeed, as early as in the *Essay of Dramatick Poesy* (1668), Lisideius commends the Frenchman, who ' so interweaves truth with probable fiction, that he puts a pleasing fallacy upon us, mends the intrigues of Fate, and dispenses with the severity of history to reward the virtue which has been rendered to us there unfortunate'. Similarly, in the preface to the much later

Don Sebastian, Dryden claimed to have apportioned misfortune according to poetic justice, letting Sebastian off the death penalty, as his crime had been involuntary. Whether or no Rymer has the precedence in invention, at any rate he put the idea clearly:

> These ['our Sophocles and Euripides'] were for teaching by examples, in a graver way, yet extremely pleasant and delightful. And finding in history the same end happen to the righteous and to the unjust, virtue often opprest, and wickedness on the throne, they saw these particular yesterday-truths were imperfect and unproper to illustrate the universal and eternal truths by them intended. Finding also that this unequal distribution of rewards and punishments did perplex the wisest, and by the atheist was made a scandal to the divine providence, they concluded that a poet must of necessity see justice exactly administered, if he intended to please. For, said they, if the world can scarce be satisfied with God Almighty, whose Holy will and purposes are not to be comprehended, a poet, in these matters, shall never be pardoned, who, they are sure, is not incomprehensible, whose ways and walks may without impiety be penetrated and examined.

In this we hear some notes already familiar, especially that which suggests that the function of the poet is to rectify God's handiwork, a note which occurs again in the next romantic revival, when the poet assumed the prophet's mantle, defiantly in Blake, complacently in Wordsworth. The idea of yesterday-truth and eternal truth is a profound one, but unfortunately the poets insisted rather on making the truth of to-day important, and ignoring eternal truth, which is not so easy to swallow. The justice of Greek tragedy is something which broods greatly above men (to put aside arguments as to the relevance of justice to tragedy); but in Restoration tragedy we are more likely to see triumph the little justice of little men. Virtue must be rewarded here and now: Aureng-Zebe must have his throne and his In'damora because he is so good a son (there is no need to multiply examples from little-read plays); and this it is which finally explains the prevalence of happy endings. The idea of poetic justice thus treated deprives tragedy of its element of exploration: men no longer tested themselves against life, as they did in Elizabethan days, since they ceased to invent horrors to stand up against.

Plot.

This theory, naturally, had a great effect upon plot. And here a distinction may usefully be made, and was perhaps on the way to being made by some of the writers of those days, between the fable and the plot, that is, between the story and the structure. Rymer, though he spoke of 'the plot or fable' as if they were the same thing, yet seems to have been aware of the distinction, but only in a vague way; and it was left to Milton to state, or re-state, it most plainly, which he did in the preface to *Samson Agonistes*, where he speaks of 'that commonly called the plot, whether intricate or explicit, which is nothing indeed but such economy, or disposition of the fable as may stand best with verisimilitude and decorum'. That was helpful; but, to comment on the last phrase, it was decorum that established itself, while verisimilitude blew away with any wind that happened to be inspiring the poet. The question of what decorum was, and of how in the very name of verisimilitude it utterly subdued and trampled it down, leads straight to the consideration of the 'unities'.

But before passing to plot, it may be as well to say a word about the fable, the story, which, in spite of all the character-mongers, Aristotle was right in considering the most important part of tragedy. 'In a tragedy they do not act to portray characters; they include the characters for the sake of the action'. Indeed, if plot is dependent upon character, then the tragedy illustrates the particular, or yesterday, and not the general or eternal truth. And tragedy, we may repeat, is not concerned with what men are nor with how they behave, but with what happens to mankind. But we may approach the subject by another road than that of the spectator, namely from that of the creative artist.

It may be assumed, from reasons which need not be attempted here, that at some period in the process of creation the poet is convinced that things are thus and thus, and not otherwise. This is his intuition. He then proceeds to find symbols to clothe his intuitions with; and for the dramatist the symbol must be a story, it cannot be a person. To write a Theophrastean 'character' of Lear would in no way have accomplished Shakespeare's purpose: it is what happened to Lear that is important. Character, of course, is necessary, but it is not the essential part of the drama; it is necessary only to give the main symbol flesh and blood, to make live the dry bones which express the intuition. The conception of character being the playwright's object has vitiated, not only criticism, but also playwriting, for longer than it is agreeable to think. Whether the Restoration tragedy writers too much ignored character, in our sense, whether they wrote too much a tragedy of humours, where people had to speak and act 'in character', and so failed to make their symbols real, is beside the point. As a matter of fact, or opinion, they did; and an absence of subtlety, or, in the modern jargon, a lack of psychology, is what they can most justly be reproached with. Nevertheless, Dryden and Otway certainly possessed 'psychology', if the lesser writers did not. But what lesser writers ever do?

Whatever the reasons, and it was only partly allegiance to Aristotle, the Restoration writers regarded plot as ' the soul of tragedy '. One meets the phrase in more than one writer. And, using the word plot in the Miltonic sense, the object of plot was to make the fable pleasing, and to endow it with verisimilitude. In what way the fable was to be made pleasing we have already seen: whether its sole object was to please is a point which was furiously discussed, as will appear later. The immediate question then, is verisimilitude. How was a play to be as like life as the use of verse would allow? The answer came pat, far too pat; by making it happen all in one place, so that you did not have to imagine yourself transported on a magic carpet; and as far as possible within the compass of three hours, for you could not imagine a man wearing the same suit of clothes for ten or twenty years. In fact, the unities, or, as Milton would have said, decorum.

The Unities.

How far the unities may be useful will be touched upon in the ' Cleopatra ' chapter; here we are concerned with the Restoration attitude: and, as usual, it is Dryden who gives us the best exposition of the varying points of view, with practical illustrations. His answer to the problem, one need hardly say, went to further issues than the ones suggested above; his was a general appeal to the sense of order. But for the moment we will cleave to a consideration of the unities as aids to illusion. How the unities came to be mixed up with the question of illusion is, as Verrall remarked, one of the curiosities of literary evolution. The maintainers of the theory appealed to Aristotle (who, as Dryden very well knew, said nothing but the most general things about two of the unities), and rested their argument for verisimilitude upon the ancients, who did not care a fig for the matter. It would be interesting to trace when and where the idea of illusion, or delusion, crept into the drama, for it appears to have been full-grown in Elizabethan days, so much so that Ben Jonson, in a phrase curiously forestalling Coleridge's famous pronouncement, warns us that in a play 'to many things a man should owe but a temporary belief, and suspension of his own judgement'. Dryden, in the *Defence of the Essay of Dramatick Poesy*, refers without hesitation to 'the belief of fiction '.

The argument round and about the unities crops up throughout the *Essay of Dramatick Poesy*. Crites, Sir Robert Howard, begins it by ascribing their perfected development to the French. The reason for the unity of time is, he declares, 'obvious to every one': the time of a play should be proportioned as near as can be to the time of the supposed action. His reason for maintaining the unity of place is equally dogmatic: since the theatre is only one place, it is unnatural to think it many. If the newly invented painted scenes might help an audience to overcome this limitation, the places so put before it must not be so far apart that it could not go there in the time allowed by the changing of the scenes. Following him, Eugenius, Lord Buckhurst, merely says that the unities of time and place are to be found neither in Greek criticism nor in Greek plays: yet he assumes that Euripides confined himself to one day, and objects to the absurdity he is guilty of on one occasion when he would have us imagine a march, a fight, and a messenger's run to take place within the space of a chorus: 'the chorus have but thirty-six verses; which is not for every mile a verse.' Lisideius, Sir Charles

Sedley, after noting how well the French observe the unities, goes on to say :

> On the other side, if you consider the historical plays of Shakespeare, they are rather so many chronicles of kings, or the business many times of thirty or forty years, crampt into a representation of two hours and a half, which is not to imitate or paint nature, but rather to draw her in miniature, to take her in little ; to look through the wrong end of a perspective [telescope], and receive her images not only much less, but infinitely more imperfect than the life. This, instead of making a play delightful, renders it ridiculous.
>
> Quodcunque ostendis mihi sic, incredulus odi.*
>
> For the spirit of man cannot be satisfied but with truth, or at least verisimility ; and a poem is to contain, if not τὰ ἔτυμα yet ἐτύμοισιν ὁμοῖα,† as one of the Greek poets has expressed it.

Neander, Dryden himself, is the only speaker in the dialogue to resent the tyranny of the unities of time and place, arguing that too close attention to the former brings about dearth of plot, for ' how many beautiful accidents might naturally happen in two or three days, which cannot arrive with any probability in the compass of twenty-four hours ? ' There the romantic jumps out of the classical cage, which needs compression for the synthesis at which it aims. For Dryden, time was ' to be allowed also for maturity of design '. As to cleaving to one place, this led to too many absurdities, increased by the necessity of binding together each scene so as never to leave the stage empty ; which last, however, obtains his grudging approval, as it does the more hearty suffrage of the others.

The argument seems barren to us now, when conducted on those lines ; verisimilitude, truth to nature, does not reside in these ' mechanic parts ' ; but a contention still

---

* Anything that you set thus before my eyes, rouses disbelief and abhorrence. Horace, *Ars Poetica*.

† If not *the truth*, yet *things like the truth*. *Odyssey*, xix. 203.

interestingly alive is that of unity of the fable, the introduction of sub-plots, and of comic relief. The three first
speakers in the *Essay* all favour unity : if there is a sub-plot,
this means that there are two plays instead of one : the
mind is distracted by too many events; or in the case of
comic relief, the emotions are put at war with each other,
for ' are not mirth and compassion incompatible ? ' Howard
had developed this in his *Preface to Four New Plays* (1665),
where he stated :

> I am now convinced in my own judgement, that it is most
> proper to keep the audience in one entire disposition both of
> concern and attention ; for when scenes of so different natures
> immediately succeed one another, 'tis probable the audience
> may not recollect themselves as to start into an enjoyment of
> the mirth or into a concern for the sadness.

Dryden, however, stoutly took the other side. He complained that French plays were too rigid ; they lacked the
quick turns and graces of the English. The matter being
short, the speechifying became tedious ; ' those long haran-
gues were introduced to comply with the gravity of a
churchman '. But ' Grief and passion are like floods, raised
in a little brook by a sudden rain . . . but a long, sober shower
gives them leisure to run out as they came in, without
troubling the ordinary current '. Dryden, in fact, was
always willing to be deluded in this, as in any other events
upon the stage ; and could as well persuade himself that
stage blows were given in earnest, as that Kynaston in the
play was Mahomet Boabdelin in Granada. As to comic
relief;

> Why should he [Lisideius] imagine the soul of man more
> heavy than his senses ? Does not the eye pass from an un-
> pleasant object to a pleasant, in a much shorter time than is
> required to this ? And does not the unpleasantness of the first
> commend the beauty of the latter ? The old rule of logic might

have convinced him, that contraries when placed near, set off
each other. A continued gravity keeps the spirit too much
bent; we must refresh it sometimes, as we bait in a journey,
that we may go on with greater ease.

The argument really is valueless, though it would be
uncivil to cast a slur upon so ancient and honourable a rule
of logic, nevertheless it represents Dryden's attitude at the
moment. He was to change his point of view and write according to the rules, reluctantly to change back again because
the public would have none of them. He was always ready,
quite reasonably, to give the public what it wanted, and
as early as the *Defence of an Essay of Dramatick Poesy* (1668)
noted that it is not always pleased with good plays, and
that plays which please it are not always good. The *Defence*
adds little to Dryden's arguments, but it clarifies them a
great deal. Howard, in his *Preface to The Great Favourite*
(1668), had attacked the *Essay* on all the subjects under
dispute, and with regard to the unities of time and place
made the point that if you can compress twenty-four hours
into three, or make the stage, which is one place, represent
several, then you need stop at nothing, since if you do, you
admit that there can be degrees of impossibility. Fancy
alone, Dryden answered, is prepared to do anything: it
will leap over times and climes to any extent; but reason
is there to check its extravagancies. The result is odd:

> There is a greater vicinity in nature, betwixt two rooms than
> betwixt two houses, betwixt two houses than betwixt two cities,
> and so of the rest; reason therefore can sooner be led by imagina-
> tion to step from one room into another, than to walk to two
> distant houses, and yet rather to go thither, than to fly like
> a witch through the air. . .

The argument as regards place 'may easily be applied to
that of time':

> For as place, so time relating to a play, is either imaginary
> or real: the real is comprehended in those three hours, more

or less, in the space of which the play is represented: the imaginary is that which is supposed to be taken up in the representation, as twenty-four hours more or less. Now no man could ever suppose that twenty-four real hours could be included in the space of three: but where is the absurdity of affirming that the feigned business of twenty-four imagined hours may not more naturally be represented in the compass of three real hours, than the like feigned business of twenty-four years in the same proportion of real time? For the proportions are always real, and much nearer, . . . of twenty-four to three, than of four thousand to it.

This argument also is unconvincing; but what always saved Dryden was his superb common sense, and his persistent refusal to be doctrinaire. He was always ready to see how the thing worked out. Here, however, we may observe a comment made by Verrall on the second of the above passages. 'This, of course, is all nonsense', he says. No writer, he argues, attempts to *compress* the events of any time, whether twenty-four hours or four thousand, into three; he *selects*. The answer is, that to compress was just what Dryden and his fellows in heroic drama, did do. Battles are fought, dynasties triumph and fall, emotions become torrential and sink again, in the short space of three hours. They might just as well, since twenty-four would not suffice for a tithe of the things which happen. And this, to make a digression in parenthesis, may account for the amazing prevalence of love at first sight, or at least of the *coup de foudre*, in these plays. *Aureng-Zebe* alone is a good instance of devastating suddenness of Cupid's shafts in that atmosphere: there was no time for the normal, tedious process. The same observation may be made of the sudden bitter hatreds of life-long friends, as for instance, in Lee's *Constantine the Great*. It really was a matter of compression, not of selection. Whether one method is better than the other depends simply upon who handles it. Criticism follows creation; it rarely imposes upon it, though it may serve as an aid to selection.

Morality.

Enough has now been quoted to orientate the content and the setting of Restoration tragedy : there now remains, before we proceed to touch upon the drama itself, the question of its purpose, whether to please or improve, which may be treated briefly. Something has already been said upon this subject when discussing those writers who declared that heroic tragedy had for aim the setting an example to great men, but the alternative was not there touched upon. The issue had been revived by Ben Jonson :

> The ends of all who for the scene do write
> Are, or should be, to profit and delight,

of which Shadwell destroyed both the subtlety and the amiable malice by saying

> If poets aim at nought but to delight,
> Fiddlers have to the bays an equal right :

from which, apart from hints elsewhere, it may be deduced that the school of art for art's sake was already in existence. But even if art does not exist for morality, there are still two possibilities : it may exist for the mere pleasure which is a form of forgetfulness of life ; or it may exist for representing life more 'lively' than it is to be seen every day, letting it have the same effect upon the recipient as life itself. In the latter instance, what counts is not the subject-matter of art, but the artistry. This was the position brilliantly taken up by Robert Wolseley in his *Preface to Valentinian* (1685). But if no subject is to be taboo, yet the artist has responsibilities, for 'as an ill poet will depress and disgrace the highest, so a good one will raise and dignify the lowest'. Wolseley does not elucidate any further, but it is clear that he had got beyond the shallower conception of art which accepts as valid the dichotomy of pleasure and profit. The benefit of art is something too subtle to be so easily pigeon-holed: we know it is a necessity; and we find that if it lends itself purposely either to pleasure or to profit, it ceases to enjoy that independent activity without which it can be of no value at all. To 'raise and dignify' may sound dangerously heroic; but it is 'the lowest' which is to be thus treated.

Wolseley was on the right track even if he did not go very far along it: at any rate, he did not fall into either of the traps. Pleasure-seekers no doubt there were; there still are, and it is to be hoped there always will be; but it is a confusion, common enough to-day, to want art to be 'fun' and to be 'jolly', just as it was a confusion on Collier's part to declare in the very first sentence of his famous and amusing polemic (1698), that 'The business of plays is to recommend virtue, and discountenance vice'. Blackmore had stated that view more fully and skilfully in the *Preface to Prince Arthur* (1695), where he said:

> 'Tis true, indeed, that the end of poetry is to give pleasure and delight; but this is a subordinate, subaltern end, which is it self a means to the greater and ultimate one before mentioned [to give men right and just conceptions of religion and virtue, &c.:] ... They are men of little genius, of mean and poor design, that employ their wit for no higher purpose than to please the imagination of vain and wanton people.

Dryden, as we shall see, knew and stated that no play could possibly profit unless it also delighted, and he made it his business to delight. The matter really is simple enough: in effect, nothing does permanently please unless it also profits, which it will not do unless it is the issue of some valuable experience. Dennis, who was the only man to answer Collier at all satisfactorily, got near this, when, in *The Usefulness of the Stage*, he argued that the theatre tends to happiness, the universal end of mankind, because it rouses the passions, which alone give pleasure. But lasting pleasure is only to be got from passions which do not conflict with reason—and these are the virtuous passions. Whether what the whole being judges to be profitable is always what the moralists think ought to be so, is, of course, a different question. It is not to be settled by any tests as yet available, for value is a ticklish thing to tackle ; and who are the vain and wanton it is difficult to decide. Delight, but this is what the Blackmores and Colliers never see, may itself be a positive value.

The whole matter, however, is only of interest as regards the criticism of the period, and not its tragic writing ; any poet who respects himself looks upon the truth at which he is aiming as superior to any moralist's truth. Attacks of morality may kill, they cannot create ; and historically, it is doubtful if the Collier controversy altered anything but the most insignificant details.

The Practice.

We may now leave criticism, and turn to the general course taken by the playwrights themselves. Not that all matters have been touched upon. It would, for instance, be singularly fruitless to dally with the question of the chorus, which Rymer advocated, and Dennis stood out against. It must be understood that a history of the criticism of the period has not been attempted ; all that has been done is to indicate its main lines.* We shall, however, return to the extremes of the common-sense attitude, and note the revulsion against 'poetic justice', when speaking

* The curious may refer to the thorough examination made by Dr. Spingarn in his introduction to *Seventeenth Century Critical Essays*.

of *Cato*. In the meantime the tragedy of the period was performing its cycle, altering and adapting itself to suit the needs of the age, or at any rate finding writers that would suit it. The general evolution will only be very lightly sketched in here, since the sort of thing which happened is heavily enough illustrated when treating separately of the chief dramatists.

It has already been hinted, and indeed, the result might have been foreseen from the first, that the materials used in Restoration tragedy degenerated into sentimentality. The gloriously abstract principles of Hobbes and Davenant were forgotten by the playwrights, who, in trying to humanize the drama, brought it nearer to life, and so turned a not indefensible unreality into falsity. This did not occur with Dryden, who was on his guard against it, and it is not very apparent in Lee. But it is visible in the younger playwrights, as well in their treatment of heroism as in their treatment of love, in both of which something of a redeeming starkness gradually ebbed away. The theory upon which the earlier writers worked was fairly water-tight, but to continue to use its subject-matter while departing from it in spirit was to court disaster. The playwrights ceased to desire heroism so greatly as to believe in it, but they went on writing as though they still did believe in it. The result is a too obvious softness. Otway, indeed, was so much a sentimentalist that sentimentalism almost becomes an admirable quality in his work, but even he seems to have felt that bone was lacking, and in *Venice Preserv'd* supplied it in the form of satirical comedy : or at any rate, even if he included the farcical scenes at the king's request, he did not feel that they were amiss as part of his structure. The scenes may appear a little too harsh for modern taste, but something of the nature was needed ; and though virility seems hardly the word to describe these exhibitions of revolting decadence, they make possible the conception of a virile element lying between the two extremes. Southerne appears to have been aware of the danger of softness, and in *Oroonoko* alternated his 'noble savage' heroism, which was Mrs. Behn's 'improvement' on the heroism of the Incas, with scenes of Restoration comedy. The public may also have felt the need for something astringent, since it was not yet ready for the frankly sentimental in either tragedy or comedy. There was evidently a struggle to maintain a balance; and this is significant, as it shows that towards the end of the century the admiration-cum-love-pity mixture was felt to be inadequate. Dryden, indeed, in the preface to *Don Sebastian* (1689), went so far as to say that he wrote with pains, 'having observed how difficult it was to please; that the humours of comedy were almost spent; that love and honour (the mistaken topics of tragedy) were quite worn out; . . . . I am still condemned to dig in those exhausted mines.' And, apparently, criticism began to fail the heroic theory here, for it turned away its interest from technical points, from materials and structure, to morality with Blackmore and Collier, and to higher aesthetics with Wolseley and Dennis.

Thus, criticism apart, we are not surprised when we come to the modification exhibited by Rowe. Heroism is by no means so heavily stressed, and not so much is made of love, though it is still the most important theme, even if the approach to it is very different, almost a revulsion in mood. Rowe also had to dig in the exhausted mines. The theory was still at work, though more weakly. Theory, of course, is not really imposed intellectually from without; it is as natural a product of the desires of the time as the works of art themselves. That an attitude does not appear in criticism, but only in practice, is no proof that it is dead. The decay may also have been partly due to the school of Rymer, who remarked that 'The end of all is to show virtue in triumph', for poetic justice was also natural truth, so long as nature was ordered: as, of course, it was. We are approaching 'whatever is, is right'.

It may also have been to some degree, the influence of Racine, which brought about the declension, for the authors of those days did not seem to realize that only Racine could write Racinian tragedies. *Cato* was a reaction against this tendency to write Racine in English, and is interesting because it is at once the last flicker of Restoration tragedy, and a breaking away from it. To us it seems much of its period; but to Addison's contemporaries it must have seemed, indeed we know it did seem, strikingly original. For what had happened to love? It takes a most insignificant place; one feels it is only dragged in because no play could be altogether without it. With *Cato*, in fact, we may say that we come to the end of heroic drama, for heroism had become a formula, and was no longer a need of the age. The Duke of Marlborough supplied what the reigns of the Stuart kings had lacked. Cato is enough of a hero, certainly, but he is a moral, not a passionate one. The play was in this way also a reaction against the sentimentality that had destroyed heroic drama, but it did not succeed in going back to heroism. If it can be said to explore life, it explores it in a way very different from that of *Almanzor and Almahide*. It was also written with a deliberate intent to defy poetic justice. Thus, if it seems from our point of view to complete the cycle, it can also be taken as the end of the period, by its showing a complete break-away from one of its most cherished notions.

III

BLANK VERSE AND THE HEROIC COUPLET

General Remarks.

ALTHOUGH it is not just to give the name of ' heroic ' only to those plays that are written in the rhyming couplet, the latter did at one period count for much in the heroic play. It was, moreover, the object of high controversy, both on practical and abstract grounds; whether, for instance, it fatigued the ear, or whether it was too far removed from life. No one, however, thought of considering it merely as an instrument of speech, as something apart from poetry meant to be read : the couplets of *Cooper's Hill* were to be judged in exactly the same way as those of *Aureng-Zebe*. But if consideration of the subject is to be of any value to us to-day, it is necessary to make the distinction.

It is easy enough to make : it is clear that the antithetical couplet, as finally perfected by Pope, would be intolerable on the stage. The attention one gives to a written poem is not the same that one gives to a speech in the theatre : it is more concentrated : everytning outside it is rigorously excluded. A speech on the stage does not only need to be less intense, it cannot afford to be so close, though pithiness is a quality it disregards at its peril. Pithiness, indeed, was what the writers of the heroic couplet largely aimed at. ' That benefit I consider most in it ', Dryden wrote in the ' Epistle Dedicatory ' of *The Rival Ladies*, beginning an argument he was to pursue as Neander in the *Essay of Dramatick Poesy*,

> . . . is, that it bounds and circumscribes the fancy. For imagination in a poet is a faculty so wild and lawless, that like

an high-ranging spaniel, it must have clogs tied to it, lest it out-run the judgement. The great easiness of blank verse renders the poet too luxuriant; he is tempted to say many things, which might better be omitted, or at least shut up in fewer words: but when the difficulty of artful rhyming is interposed, where the poet commonly confines his sense to the couplet, and must contrive his sense into such words, that the rhyme shall naturally follow them, not they the rhyme, the fancy then gives leisure to the judgement to come in; which seeing so heavy a tax imposed, is ready to cut off all unnecessary expenses.

This is not really at odds with what he develops in the *Essay*, that verse may be a great help to a luxuriant fancy, since there also it is only made an aid because it gives time for second thoughts, for the judgement, to enter in.

The point, to which we shall return, is that blank verse is too luxuriant; it sometimes ' runs on for so many lines together, that the reader is out of breath to overtake it '. But to keep to the distinction which we want to make here, namely between verse that is read and verse that is heard, one must insist that the couplet in its extreme form will not do for the stage. In read verse, confining the sense to the couplet was only the first step: after that, each line had to be separated into balancing halves, and these halves themselves had to correspond antithetically with each other :

> Just hint a fault, and hesitate dislike.

Nor did English verse have to wait for Pope to reach this development, though it was he who applied the principle with least mercy. Denham himself had indicated it :

> Strong without rage, without o'erflowing full;

and, Waller apart, Dryden used the instrument most skil-fully when he wished :

> Without unspotted, innocent within,
> She feared no danger, for she knew no sin.

It is clear that the medium is too stiff, one might almost say too brittle, to carry the rapid changes of passion natural to the stage. No instance of it in Restoration tragedy comes to the memory, though Mr. Lytton Strachey has pulled out a plum from *Othello*.

> She that could think, and ne'er disclosed her mind;
> See suitors following, and not look behind;
> She was a wight, if ever such wights were,
> To suckle fools, and chronicle small beer.

For stage speech is not pure literature; it is a form of oratory meant to move an audience as well as to imitate conversation. As a good stage instrument it should be flexible and bring the stress on the word that is meant to strike home. It must admit of great variation in pace, so as to express excitement or brooding sorrow, haste or dalliance, in fact the whole gamut of the emotions. The antithetical couplet is obviously too rigid, and even the ordinary dramatic couplet is expected to do things outside its possible scope. In this passage from Lee's *The Tragedy of Nero*, the rhythm is called upon to express at least four different emotions:

Nero.   That you the Prince your brother's blood would spill;
No matter how, so you but swear to kill.
Here with my dagger let the deed be done:
You often find him sleeping and alone.

Octavia.   Sleeping! Oh Gods! Can you your vengeance keep?
Where is your thunder? No, 'tis you that sleep.
Sure else your justice would his vice confound,
And drive this monster quick into the ground.
Hell to his soul such impudence has giv'n,
That he in time will storm your fort of Heaven:
In blasphemies his spirits do exhale;
Your high bright walls his giant crimes will scale.
Oh, my heart's full.

Nero.   Here's that will give it vent: (*Stabs*
So now go tell the Gods my black intent.   *her.*)

Britannicus his death I will defer;
'Tis pretty well I've made an end of her.
Now will I haste to meet Poppea's arms:
Oh, Love, assist me with thy mighty charms. . .
Octavia. Oh, my Britannicus, my brother!—oh,
Might I but see thee once, yet e'er I go,
And wander in the wide dark dens of death :
But, oh! my soul is almost out of breath.   (II. iii.)

The somewhat ludicrous result is not altogether Lee's fault, except that he chose the medium.

Dryden himself was quite aware of this defect in the couplet form, though he did not analyse the 'monotony' in that way. In the preface to *Tyrranick Love* he said, 'I have not everywhere observed the equality of numbers in my verse; partly by reason of my haste; but more especially because I would not have my sense a slave to syllables.' In more than one place he draws attention to his custom of leaving certain lines incomplete, and outside the rhyme system, so as to allow the ear the ease of variety; and, carrying this idea over into his later blank verse, he would have his readers note 'the roughness of the numbers and cadences' in *Don Sebastian*. How flexible the rhymed medium might become under Dryden's hand may well be illustrated from *Tyrranick Love* itself, in a passage which contains, moreover, an antithetical line not far removed from one of those quoted out of *The Hind and Panther*, as well as the occasional alexandrine he used:

Damilcar. Mercy, bright Spirit; I already feel
The piercing edge of thy immortal steel :
Thou, Prince of day, from elements art free :
And I all body when compared to thee.
Thou tread'st th' Abyss of Light !
And where it streams with open eye can'st go :
We wander in the fields of air below :
Changelings and fools of heav'n: and thence shut out,

> Wildly we roam in discontent about:
> Gross-heavy-fed, next Man in ignorance and sin,
> And spotted all without, and dusky all within,
> Without thy sword I perish by thy sight,
> I reel, and stagger, and am drunk with light.   (IV.)

Certainly there we never feel that rhyme is dictating to sense, or even that the sense is being hampered. To what Coleridge called 'the known effects of metre', are added what we might call 'the known effects of rhyme' (only every one will not admit them), working in the same direction. Each line has a reason for submitting to the form: but it is a rhetorical, not a purely poetic reason. The form of the heroic couplet is not that of the couplet as consummated by Pope.

The Controversy.

With this point clear, we may pass to the battle over rhyme which enlivened criticism for some twenty years, a battle seen at its richest in the duel between Dryden and Sir Robert Howard. It began in the *Essay of Dramatick Poesy*, where Neander (Dryden) defends rhyme against the attacks of Crites (Howard). Dryden had evidently read Howard's *Preface to Four New Plays* (1665) before writing his Essay (in 1666?), though he probably also gathered the substance in conversation. However it may be, Dryden presents Howard's argument not only more agreeably, but more convincingly than Howard himself does; except that, by taking his argument one logical step further, he shows its falsity. The line Howard took was that when an actor caps a fellow-actor's rhyme, 'the smartness of a reply, which has its beauty by coming from sudden thoughts, seems lost by that which rather looks like a design of two than the answer of one.' Or, as Crites said, 'Now what is more unreasonable than to imagine, that a man should not only imagine the wit, but the rhyme too upon the sudden? This nicking of him who spoke before both in sound and measure, is so great in happiness, that you must at least suppose the persons of your play to be born poets.' Dryden's reply was that a good writer might make a rhyme sound as natural as anything else, or at any rate as blank verse, ' by the well placing of the words, etc.'. Of course, if a man was not a good poet, he had better steer clear of any kind of verse. Verse, as he insisted in the *Essay*, was only admissible if it could be made to sound natural.

In his *Preface to The Great Favourite* (1668) Howard recklessly attacks Dryden, 'and ' cannot . . . but beg leave of the reader to take a little notice of the great pains the author of an *Essay of Dramatick Poesy* has taken to prove rhyme as natural in a serious play, and more effectual than blank verse.' Dryden, he says, has mistaken the sense of the word natural; 'for 'tis not the question whether rhyme or not rhyme be the best or most natural for a grave and serious subject, but what is the nearest the nature of that which it presents.' Dryden, the gloves being off, replied vigorously in his *Defence of an Essay of Dramatick Poesy* (1668), where he trounced Howard severely and entertainingly for his slips and mistranslations. He had no difficulty, of course, in making Howard look silly with respect to the last sentence of his: 'I wonder he should think me so ridiculous as to dispute whether prose or verse be nearest to ordinary conversation.' The point is one of art, not of life; that is whether verse ' be natural or not in plays '.

He at once gets on to the real point. It is not at bottom a question of the natural at all: ' I am satisfied if it cause delight: for delight is the chief, if not the only end of poesy; instruction can be admitted but in the second place, for poesy only instructs as it delights.' Thus in *Biographia*

Literaria (it is astonishing how often one is reminded of Coleridge when reading Dryden); ' A poem is that species of composition, which is opposed to works of science, by proposing for its *immediate* object, pleasure, not truth.' And the *Defence* continues, that since the poet's business is ' to affect the soul, and excite the passions, and above all to move admiration (which is the delight of serious plays), a bare imitation will not serve.' Howard states that a play is ' supposed to be the composition of several persons speaking extempore:' Dryden begs to differ: ' a play is supposed to be the work of a poet.' He imitates, certainly, but imitation in this sense, we have seen, means feigning, making as if. On the other hand, he declares that the objection to prose is precisely that it is too like life. The proper ' heightening ' is not attained. ' Thus prose, though the rightful prince, yet is by common consent deposed, as too weak for the government of serious plays.' He goes on to take up the point Howard had made from Aristotle, that tragedies should be written in the verse which is nearest prose. For Howard, the verse of the ancients was blank verse, but Dryden argues that rhyme in modern verse replaces measure in the ancient: that if the ancients were to write tragedy now, they would certainly use rhyme, as being ' most remote from conversation '.

His real plea is made in *An Essay on Heroick Plays* (1671):

Whether heroic verse ought to be admitted into serious plays, is not now to be disputed; it is already in possession of the stage, and I dare confidently affirm, that very few tragedies, in this age, shall be received without it. All the arguments which are formed against it, can amount to no more than this, that it is not so near conversation as prose, and therefore not so natural. But it is very clear to all who understand poetry, that serious plays ought not to imitate conversation too nearly. If nothing were to be raised above that level, the foundation of poetry would be destroyed. And if you once admit of a latitude, that thoughts may be exalted, and that images and actions may be raised above the life, and described in measure without rhyme, that leads you insensibly from your principles to mine : you are already so far onward of your way, that you have forsaken the imitation of ordinary converse. You are gone beyond it ; and to continue where you are, is to lodge in the open fields, betwixt two inns. You have lost that which you call natural, and have not acquired the last perfection of art... It is indeed so difficult to write verse, that the adversaries of it have a good plea against many, who undertook that task, without being formed by art or nature for it. Yet, even they who have written worst in it, would have written worse without it : they have cozened many with their sound, who never took pains to examine their sense. In fine, they have succeeded ; though it is true they have more dishonoured rhyme by their good success, than they have done by their ill. But I am willing to let fall this argument : it is free for every man to write, or not to write, in verse, as he judges it to be, or not to be his talent ; or as he imagines the audience will receive it.

The last is in direct contradiction to Howard's ' the dispute is not which way a man may write best in, but which is most proper for the subject he writes upon '. It was not Dryden's way thus to pre-judge a cause.

The Quatrain.

With Dryden's admirable piece of theoretical criticism, we also may be willing to let fall the argument, and turn for a moment to the practice. Time was to falsify his prophesy, and blank verse soon regained its sway, even with Dryden himself. But it is possible that Dryden, though he argued brilliantly for it, was not quite happy with it as a stage instrument. It is exceedingly hard to avoid monotony in the couplet, and the expected rhyme, instead of rousing the attention, as often as not lulls it to indifference. There were ways in which its worst effects could be avoided ; one could insert a triplet here and there, use a single imperfect line to break the unified front, drop into an alexandrine or two, and above all, there was the quatrain to play with. Of this Davenant had given the recent example, for it is doubtful if the writers of the age paid much attention to Daniel's *Cleopatra*, or to Greene's *Selimus*, and the quatrain is practically absent from Shakespeare, it occurs in *Romeo and Juliet*, and may be met with in *Richard II*, III. ii.

> But now the blood of twenty-thousand men
> Did triumph in my face, and they are fled;
> And till so much blood thither come again,
> Have I not reason to look pale and dead?

Dryden toyed with it, with an effect which is full of charm in the study: but the charm itself—and this is a notion which the Restoration does not seem to have chanced on—may detract from the dramatic quality. The quatrain might have done admirably in *The Faithful Shepherdess*, but it tended to sentimentalize tragedy. An instance of it may be given from *The Indian Emperor* (I. ii):

Cortez. To make me happier than that wish can do,
    Lies not in all your Gods to grant, but you;
    Let this fair princess but one minute stay,
    A look from her will your obligements pay.

Montezuma. (*To Cydaria*) Your duty in your quick return be shown,
    Stay you, and wait my daughter to the town.
            (*Exeunt omnes except Cortez, Cydaria and guards.*)

Cydaria.   My father's gone, and yet I cannot go,
    Sure I have something lost, or left behind. (*Aside*)

Cortez.   Like travellers who wander in the snow,
    I on her beauty gaze 'till I am blind. (*Aside*)

Cydaria.   Thick breath, quick pulse, and heaving of my heart,
    All signs of some unwonted change appear:
    I find myself unwilling to depart,
    And yet I know not why I would be here
      Stranger, you raise such torments in my breast,

> That when I go (if I must go again),
>   I'll tell my father you have robbed my rest,
> And to him of your injuries complain.
> *Cortez.*   Unknown, I swear, those wrongs were which I
>   wrought,
> But my complaints will much more just appear,
>   Who from another world my freedom brought,
> And to your conquering eyes have lost it here.
> *Cydaria.*   Where is that other world from whence you came?
> *Cortez.* Beyond the ocean, far from hence it lies.
> *Cydaria.*   Your other world, I fear, is then the same
> That souls must go to when the body dies.
>   But what's the cause that keeps you here with me,
> That I may know what keeps me here with you?
> *Cortez.*   Mine is a love which must perpetual be,
> If you can be so just as I am true.
>   (*Enter Orbellan.*)
> *Orbellan.* Your father wonders much at your delay.
> *Cydaria.* So great a wonder for so small a stay!
> *Orbellan.* He has commanded you with me to go.
> *Cydaria.* Has he not sent to bring the stranger too?
> *Orbellan.* If he to-morrow dares in fight appear,
>   His high-placed love perhaps may cost him dear.

And so on, in couplets, for the remaining ten lines of the act. The purpose is clear, namely to bring about a change in tempo, a slowing down, which the couplet, as at that time (1665) Dryden could control it, would not admit.

Nor was Dryden alone in feeling that the couplet was too metallic, and ten years later, Edmund Phillips, in the *Preface to Theatrum Poetarum* wrote:

> . . . and for the verse, if it must needs be rhyme, I am clearly of opinion that way of versifying, which bears the name of Pindaric, and which hath no necessity of being divided into strophs or stanzas, would be much more suitable for tragedy than the continued rhapsody of rhyming couplets, which whoever shall mark it well will find it appear too stiff and of too much constraint for the liberty of conversation and the interlocution of several persons. . .

It was left to Congreve to analyse the structure of the

Pindaric ode, and find that it was after all divided into strophs or stanzas ; and one may guess that the form which Phillips was after could be found in the choruses of *Samson Agonistes*. Rymer on the other hand, objected to Davenant's quatrains on the ground that they obliged him to stretch every period to the end of four lines, to do which he had to fill up ' perpetually with parentheses, the words jumbled in confusion, and a darkness spread over all '. Nevertheless, as Settle found, the quatrain could be used quite effectively for relief, in very short stretches ; but he used it much more sparingly than Lee, who employed it often, though never for so long together as Dryden did, and keeping it fairly hard :

> Why was I destined to be born above,
> By midwife honour to the light conveyed,
> Fame's darling, the bright infant of high love,
> Crowned, and in Empire's golden cradle laid ;
> Rocked by the hand of empresses, that yield
> Their sceptres formed to rattles for my hand,
> Born to the wealth of the green floating field
> And the rich dust of all the yellow land ?

> (*Gloriana*, I. i.)

Blank Verse.

But if the couplet proved too rigid for dramatic purposes (and after all, whatever the argument, the proof of the pudding is in the eating), it did at least stop the rot which had set in in the writing of blank verse. It pruned luxuriance, certainly, but not in the sense Dryden meant it. It was not so much that it gave the judgement time to act upon the fancy, or, by working through the writers' laziness, pruned the prolix branches, as that it trained them to a standard the later Elizabethans had forgotten. No one conversant with the drama after, say, 1620, can deny that blank verse had arrived at a state of disintegration, in Middleton,

in Shirley and other equally good writers (not to descend
to Jasper Mayne and such like), who could write excellent blank verse when they chose. It had come to consist
merely of loosely strung phrases of anything from seven
to fourteen syllables, with a corresponding laxity of accent
or weight, for, of course, it is the structure of the phrase
which matters, not the number of syllables. Stage blank
verse is really only a device for giving the phrase a shape
easily manageable by people speaking to an audience, but
no one reading much of the later verse would imagine
that this was so. In this matter, however, the couplet was
rigorous, but it went too far in the other direction, and
the rhyme often has almost the effect of spoken punctuation. The couplet does not easily admit of straddling, so
that the sentences incline to be chopped off all of the same
length, which is both monotonous and inexpressive. Thus,
though most writers tried it, most of those who did so
abandoned it. But it was not without its influence on
blank verse. Much shocking blank verse was, it is true,
written after this, but it did not all at once err on the side
of looseness: the ends of the strings were all neatly tied together. This certainly was an advantage, and if the couplet
failed to justify itself as an instrument, it undoubtedly did
so as a discipline. Take Dryden's blank verse in those parts
of *Amboyna* he thought needed 'heightening' (the most
vicious conception approved by the Restoration):

> Courage, my friend, and rather praise we Heaven,
> That it has chose two such as you and me,
> Who will not shame our country with our pains,
> But stand like marble statues in their fires,
> Scorched and defaced, perhaps, not melted down.

It has a light step, far removed from the heavy tread of
pre-Shakespearian blank verse, such as Sackville's or Gas-
coigne's, but it has little flexibility. It will obviously not

carry more weight than the couplet will, not so much, in fact, as the couplet will at its best. That Dryden could do infinitely better is illustrated in other chapters.

The defeat of the couplet led to developments in blank verse which are most illuminating, though it must be borne in mind that the blank verse here discussed is that especially written for the stage, and has nothing to do with, say, that of Milton in *Paradise Lost*, which would be unendurable. The development, or change, to correspond with matter can be beautifully traced in its main outlines, though not strictly chronologically, since authors have an unlucky habit of writing as individuals, and not as members of a platoon. Some are before their time; others lag distressingly behind.

Once the common-sense reaction set in, with naturalism intruding itself under its wing, the couplet was doomed, since tragedy forfeited its superb detachment from life, its really healthy artificiality. And with naturalism, the romantic basis showed itself in the form romance always takes upon itself unless rigorously chastened by art, namely as sentimentality. With Mrs. Aphra Behn's *Oroonoko*, with the invention that is, of the noble savage, romance lost a certain cliff-like hardness, and subsided into a sea of emotions:

> Till at the last the sapped foundations fall,
> And universal ruin swallows all.

The stage was then vacant for the sentimental comedy of Cibber, Steele, and their contemporaries.

When Dryden really wrote blank verse, as in *All for Love*, he made it, as will be seen in the next chapter, into a fitting and honourable vehicle for the drama. Being the greatest stage poet of his age, far superior to the others in technique at any rate, his verse is better than that of others.

But Lee's is not too bad: at least it is not merely the vaguely cadenced prose of the late Elizabethans. To take a passage at random, from his early work, though one fairly typical of his 'meaty' manner, we may quote from the first scene of *The Massacre of Paris*:

Lorain. Speak lower.
Guise. What, upon my father's death!
O glorious Guise, be calm upon thy murder!
No, I will hollow my revenge so loud,
That his great ghost shall hear me up to Heav'n,
In height of honours. Oh, to fall so basely,
When Orleance was blocked up, and conquests crowned thee,
By damned Poltrot so villainously slain,
Poltrot, by Beza, and this curs'd admiral,
Set on with hopes of infinite rewards,
Here and hereafter, so to blast thy glory!
O, I could pull my bursting eyeballs forth,
But that they may one day prove basilisks
To that detested head of all these broils.
Then tortures, racks, and death shall close thy wound,
Kill him in riots, pride, and lust of pleasures,
That I may add damnation to the rest,
And foil his soul and body both together.

It is, of course, a little jerky, a little too end-stopped; but it is fluid and moderately flexible, and brings the stress on the right word for sense. It satisfies the main needs of stage speech; and so it was a tolerably good stage instrument. What was lacking to make it great was the mind behind it, as much as the ear which judged it.

Otway, again, in his earlier tragedies, submitted to the discipline of the rhymed couplet: but he was never easy in it, and even his best passages smack of the set poem, rather than the utterances of a living being. The exigencies of rhyme, of which he was not a skilful enough master, forced him into places where he cannot but look a little

ridiculous. Where, as with Dryden, the playwright has the
faculty of making the general statement, the more removed
effect of the couplet is admirable: but where naturalism
intrudes, especially naturalism in speech and diction, the
contrast of matter and manner is too discordant to be com-
formable. 'Nothing can permanently please', Coleridge
remarked, ' which does not contain in itself the reason
why it is so, and not otherwise.' It is not that the extra
attention induced by rhyme fails to be supported by con-
formable matter, but that the rhyme itself distracts the
attention because the word does not come pat. Moreover
the rhyme is often bad, and the verse padded to bring it off.
In short, there is no reason why most of Otway's rhymed
plays should be in that medium at all, except that Otway
thought it was the right thing, which is not a reason in the
verse itself. The ear is wantonly titillated:

T. Vesp: Oh! did my father, good Vespasian, live,
How happy should I be!
Berenice.   Ah, cease to grieve!
Your tears have reverenced his memory now.
Cares are to Rome and your own glory due.
A father you lament, a feeble grief,
Whilst for your absence I find no relief.
But in your presence only take delight,
I, who shall die, if but debarred your sight.   (I. ii.)

The medium was in reality too stern for him; but once
he allowed himself the freedom of blank verse, he became
diffuse, so diffuse, that he often let the idea be lost in verbiage which carried him into falsity, as may be seen from
his ' tame lamb' passage (see p. 143). It was partly that the
judgement did not have to trim the luxuriance of his fancy,
but also, sometimes, that he hoped that mere words would do
the work the fancy itself refused. This is not consistently
true; he was a good poet, and the thought and the emotion

behind his writings always maintained him at that level.
But we feel that with him the medium is in decline, just
as the idea of heroic tragedy is dropping with him : there
is no longer the strict correspondence of word and image
with emotion or thought that there is in Dryden, and all
the later Elizabethans. Yet it is not badly adapted to what
he wanted it to do : it lacks the strength of Lee's, but it can
allow much more readily of sentimental feeling ; and to
make this point we must choose a passage where sentimentality is not involved.

> 'Tis such a wrong as even tortures thought,
> That we, who've been her champion forty years,
> Fought all her battles with renowned success,
> And never lost her yet a man in vain,
> Should, now her noblest fortune is at stake,
> And Mithridates' sword is drawn, be thrown
> Aside, like some old broken, battered shield :
> To see my laurels wither as I rust :
> And all this managed by the cursed craft,
> Petulant envy, and malignant spite
> Of that old barking Senate's dog, Metellus.
>
> (*Caius Marius*, I. i.)

Technically it is much freer than Lee's verse, less end-
stopped ; and Otway was to become freer still, though he
never relapsed into the looseness of the late Elizabethans.
Perhaps the best proof of how practice in the couplet makes
for light and handy blank verse can be obtained from Banks,
where we get blank verse sliding into the couplet without
any feeling of change. Many used this device for shutting
the door upon an act, as though tacitly admitting that rhyme
was the more final form ; but Banks used it frequently. The
example which follows, however, is from the end of Act III
of *The Albion Queens* (1684 ; 1704).

> Prepare her table, deck the bed of state,
> Let her apartment shine with golden arras,

> Strew perfume in her way sweeter than incense,
> Rare as the sun draws every morning up,
> And fragrant as the breath upon her lips ;
> Sweet music sound where e'er she wakes or sleeps,
> Musick as sweet, harmonious, and as still,
> As does this soft and gentle bosom fill.
> Then let her go, with hand in hand combined,
> The white cross with the red thus ever joined. . .

but there, it is true, the rhyme seems definitely to add a sense of pageantry.

Decay.

The difficulty then, as now, was to find a medium to convey, without being ridiculous, all ' the highest that can be delivered in Heroic Poesy ', to quote Phillips once more, ' as being occasioned upon representing to the very life the unbridled passions of love, rage, and ambition [*præcipitandus est liber spiritus* indeed], the violent ends or down falls of great princes, the subversion of kingdoms and estates, and whatsoever can ⟨be⟩ imagined of funest or tragical, which will require a style not ramping, but passionately sedate and moving.' The passions may be unbridled, that is life ; but the words must be passionately sedate, that is art : the counsel is one of perfection. Lee undoubtedly ramped, as we have seen, and shall see again. Nobody doubted but that the end of verse was to ' heighten ' ; the difficulty was, not to blow up the tragedy too high. Thus Blackmore, no less, echoed Dryden (p. 19) in saying of poetry that

> The delicacy of its strains, the sweetness and harmony of its numbers, the lively and admirable manner of its painting or representation, and the wonderful force of its eloquence cannot but triumph over our passions, and leave behind them very deep impressions.

Thus diction was an important part of the problem, and, as Dennis said in *The Impartial Critick* (1693), 'an expres-

sion may be too bold or too florid for prose, and yet be very
becoming of verse'. The words must be worthy of 'the
greatness of the thought and the dignity of heroic verse'.
The dreadful results are obvious, and were ridiculed by
George Granville, Lord Lansdowne, in his *Essay Upon Unnatural Flights in Poetry* (1701). After speaking of 'just
proportions', he goes on:

> Who, driven with ungovernable fire,
> Or void of art, beyond the bounds aspire,
> Gigantic forms and monstrous births alone
> Produce, which nature shockt disdains to own. . .
> Such frantic flights are like a mad-man's dream,
> And nature suffers in the wild extreme.

This criticism, of course, came after the great spate of high-
falutin words : where the words are less artificial, the verse
can be more natural. Unfortunately, in verse, as in the plays
themselves, the change, which might have been full of promise, led to softness instead of to a saner handling.

One has only to look at Southerne to see this effect
taking place. His verse is often clumsy, halting, far too
often end-stopped, and sometimes its rhythm is hardly to
be distinguished from that of prose. But whenever he is at
all rich and flowing, he is apt to become pulpy. Take even
a passage which aims at strength:

> It is not always granted to the great
> To be most happy : if the angry powers
> Repent their favours, let 'em take 'em back :
> The hopes of Empire, which they gave my youth
> By making me a prince, I here resign.
> Let 'em quench in me all those glorious fires,
> Which kindled at their beams : that lust of fame,
> The fever of ambition, restless still,
> And burning with the sacred thirst of sway,
> Which they inspired, to qualify my fate,
> And make me fit to govern under them,
> Let 'em extinguish.   (*Oroonoko*, v. iv.)

If that does not seem too bad taken by itself, one has only to compare it with any passage of Dryden, or even of Lee, to see how nerveless, how boneless one may say, it then becomes. The reason really is that it lacks thought. That is what is apt to happen when poets think that poetry can be made out of the emotions alone. Otway never fell into that error; he was always striving for the marriage of thought and feeling which produces good poetry: but Southerne, with his contemporaries, took it all too easily. His verse is like an embroidered garment covering a flimsy frame.

Rowe had a far greater command of words than Southerne; his verse is more flowing, and at the same time softer still: it is more polite and sentimental, and exactly suits his polite and sentimental tragedy:

> She's gone; and as she went, ten thousand fires
> Shot from her angry eyes, as if she meant
> Too well to keep the cruel vow she made.
> Now, as thou art a man, Horatio, tell me,
> What means this wild confusion in thy looks?
> As if thou wert at variance with thy self,
> Madness and reason combating within thee,
> And thou wert doubtful which should get the better.
>
> (*The Fair Penitent*, III. i.)

It is all padding; not a thought, either general or relevant to the occasion, is struck out; it is merely an attempt to fill vacuity with ' poetic beauties '.

Finally, when we come to Addison, something very peculiar happens. Read such a passage as this, chosen almost at random:

> Cato, commit these wretches to my care,
> First let 'em each be broken on the rack,
> Then with what life remains, impaled and left
> To writhe at leisure round the bloody stake.   (III. v)

The ear is continually deceived. With astonishment we discover that Addison has been writing in a rhymed measure

without the rhymes. Although the measure would seem
most usually to fit the quatrain rhyme, what we are certain
of is that some sort of rhyme is lacking. This becomes all
the more apparent when, at the end of each act, he allows
the rhyme ingress for a few lines, and we greet them with
relief :

> Let us not, Lucia, aggravate our sorrows,
> But to the Gods permit th' event of things.
> Our lives, discoloured with our present woes,
> May still grow white, and smile with happier hours.
>
> So the pure limpid stream when foul with stains,
> Of rushing torrents, and descending rains,
> Works itself clear, and as it runs, refines ;
> 'Till by degrees, the floating mirror shines,
> Reflects each flower that on the border grows,
> And a new Heaven in its fair bosom shows.   (1.)

The heroic couplet had taken its revenge, and we see what
had come about. Just as Addison had returned to the old
form of heroic play, leaving out one element in it, so, in a
like effort to redeem the vehicle of the drama, he had returned to the old form of verse, leaving out one of its most
important factors. His verse is an object lesson in what
blank verse is not. Thus in medium, as well as in form and
matter, Addison may be said to close a phase of dramatic
writing, which had its rise under peculiar conditions, and
flickered out in *Cato* (1713) when those conditions had for
some years ceased to exist.

IV

CLEOPATRA AND 'THAT CRITICALL WARR'

A Study of Form.

'The fact that Shakespeare can make a plan succeed does not show that the plan is, abstractedly considered, a good plan.'
A. C. BRADLEY, *Shakespearean Tragedy.*

SINCE certain questions are no nearer solution to-day than they were in the seventeenth century, this chapter is an endeavour to analyse what actually happened to one subject when treated by poets whose methods differed. The problems are not merely academic ones, their discussion no idle query as to whether Shakespeare or Dryden was right: but an attempt to see how far Kaiser in *From Morn to Midnight*, O'Neill in *The Emperor Jones*, or Mr. Galsworthy in *Escape* were well advised to adopt the episodic form: or whether they would have done better to stick to the unities as Gide in *Saül*, or Mr. Shaw in *You Never Can Tell*. Again, is it not possible that the reason for Mr. C. K. Munro's *At Mrs. Beam's* being more popular than his *Progress*, is not because the former play is poetically better, which it is not, but precisely because an audience is more easily reached through the severer structure?

The form which the discussion took in the seventeenth century may well be re-stated by two quotations. Samuel Butler's position was in the nature of a romantic reaction against discipline:

> ... Measuring of air upon Pernassus
> With cylinders of torricellian glasses;
> Reduce all tragedy by rules of art
> Back to its antique theatre, a cart...

An English poet should be tried b'his peers,
And not by pedants and philosophers,
Incompetent to judge poetic fury.

Thomas Rymer's attitude was at once an answer to Butler's attack upon pedants and philosophers, and an appeal to fact:

> The truth is, what Aristotle writes on this subject are not the dictates of his own magisterial will or dry deductions of his metaphysicks: but the poets were his masters, and what was their practice he reduced to principles.

Rymer's error was to take for granted that because Aristotle's generalizations were right in regard to the plays he knew, they were necessarily so for other times and other countries; and this was the weak spot where men such as Robert Howard and Butler could attack him. It might have been wiser to ask whether Aristotle, faced with the Elizabethans, might not have had to modify his conclusions. To this, of course, he could have answered, and in part did answer, that the end of tragedy was the same as it had always been since Æschylus; that form and feeling were, though distinct, as inseparable as the Phoenix and the Turtle; and that therefore, since human nature did not change, as Racine had wisely remarked, the same formal elements would arouse the same emotions. But even so, the field of fact would have been left open.

Thus the path it seems most useful to follow is one of inquiry into how much is gained or thrown away by writing within certain limits, and whether the profit outweighs the possible loss. If *Antony and Cleopatra* is better than *All for Love*, is this due to advantages of method or of mind? And if to the latter, whether the genius of Shakespeare itself would not have benefited from the more austere discipline? for 'great forces ask great labour in the management', as Davenant aptly pronounced. Our inquiry may also be aided by referring to Daniel's *Cleopatra*, which is composed on yet another method, being the extreme English example of the Senecan form, but which nevertheless throws light on certain aspects of the others. Unfortunately Sedley's play is too viciously bad to do more than serve as a source of interesting sidelights on the currents of contemporary thought and feeling as they affected Dryden, and these are better obtained from writings considered elsewhere in this essay.

In his preface to *All for Love*, Dryden threw off the remark that the death of Antony and Cleopatra had attracted the greatest wits of our nation, adding, perhaps deliberately to exclude Jodelle and the Italians, on account of the 'excellency of the moral'. Assuming for the moment that Dryden meant what we do by 'moral', we may neglect its place in these dramas, not so much to avoid the general issue of its effect on the main result of a work of art, but because in all three plays the judgement of values is much the same. Morals there are in abundance in all three plays, especially in Daniel's; but they are by-the-way generalizations (Senecan *sententiae*), arising out of the emotions of the people who utter them, and so are portions of the fabric of each part. So in *Cleopatra*:

> For grappling in the ocean of our pride,
> We suncke others greatness both together:
> Thus doth the ever-changing course of things
> Run a perpetual circle.
>
> —Ourselves must be the cause we fall
> Although the same be first decreed on high:
> Our errors still must bear the blame of all,
> This must be; earth ask not heaven why.

These are expressions of feeling, however much they may borrow the formulas of ethics or philosophy. One of the most potent weapons of the drama is this sort of statement, and we meet it in any good drama, as, for instance, when

Ibsen in *An Enemy of the People* makes Stockmann say, ' A man should never put on his best trousers when he goes out to battle for freedom and truth.' Without such statements no drama can ever be permanent, and we may therefore pass directly to the treatment of the story.

All three poets worked on the same history, as translated by North, though Daniel may have gone to Plutarch or Amyot, and it is supposed that he studied Garnier's *Marc Antoine* : but the plot is in each case different. The directing principle of the plot we may here, to avoid confusion, call the theme, which is what Dryden meant by the moral, as is clear from the preface to *Troilus and Cressida*. Again, actions are only of value in so far as they develop the theme, and here we may distinguish between actions and events. Only those events are action which are the outcome of the emotions and needs of the protagonists, and are necessary to the tragic climax. In this sense thought may rank as action, for, to quote the *Essay of Dramatick Poesy* :

> Every alteration or crossing of design, every new-sprung passion, and turn of it, is a part of the action, and much the noblest, except we conceive nothing to be action until the players come to blows ; as if the painting of the hero's mind were not more properly the poet's work than the strength of his body.

Nobody of course, not even Settle, thought the strength of the body important except as it moulded the hero's character, but the remark was worth making. Nevertheless it is only true so long as the thoughts are not barren, and do influence the result, since, as Aristotle insisted, ' the end for which we live is a certain kind of activity, not a quality.' Indeed, we may go further than Dryden, and say that action without thought is empty, for thought defines character, without which the theme has no mainspring.

Daniel's theme is the sorrow of a woman who *has been* Cleopatra, and who, bereft of Antony, struggles between, on the one hand her desire to obtain an heritage for her children, and on the other, her horror of making a Roman holiday. She ultimately finds a refuge in death. His theme is narrowed to the utmost limit. Dryden's is the struggle between Cleopatra and the Egyptians on one side, Ventidius and Rome on the other, for Antony himself, which ends, through the natural turns of passion, in the death of the lovers: thus heroic love is only part of his theme. Shakespeare's is difficult to disentangle, being of too wide a sweep for definition. Perhaps it would be safest to say that his is merely the general tragic theme, illustrating the sort of thing which happens to mankind; but if we try to describe it, we may say it combines those of Daniel and Dryden, and adds to them a vast theme of empire. It is stretched to the furthest limit. There is, in short, no main theme to take hold of: one terrifying vision of man's need to act a part before himself seems to cover it all. Moreover, there is no distinction between the history and the plot. To read North, and then to read *Antony and Cleopatra*, is to be amazed at how little Shakespeare brought his creative activity to bear on the structure of the play. Similarly, in one character only, that of Enobarbus, has he set his imagination to work; the rest are as he found them in North. As a result, the final effect of his play hardly differs from that of North's biography, except in intensity; it is exactly the same in kind, and that kind does not seem to be that of tragedy. Whether Shakespeare was trying to produce a tragedy is another question, and beside our point: we are concerned to know not why, but how it is not one.

The Panoramic Method.

We may now plunge into 'that Criticall warr which never ceases amongst the learned', and ask how far Shakespeare was hampered by the 'panoramic' method, and what are the advantages of the unities. The virtue of that of time lies in the fact that it almost automatically cuts out all that is accidental, and thus unnecessary to the tragedy. For a tragedy, and no one will disagree with Aristotle in this, should contain only what is necessary to it, and nothing else. For if a work of art succeeds through the measure in which it arouses appetencies in us, and satisfies them, the appetency and the satisfaction must not be in excess of each other; nor must each kind of art involve more impulses than it requires for its resultant emotion. In the last analysis, the structure of a play is made up of the relation between themselves of the emotions we are made to feel. Pity and fear, the impulse to approach and the impulse to flee, Mr. I. A. Richards suggests (though we might perhaps say instead the expansive and the paralysing instincts) are those through which, maybe, tragedy produces its results. In any case, to shelve this question for the moment, whatever may be the opposing impulses through which tragedy works, hope, expectation, dread, admiration, the sense of conflict and so on, are only the technical tricks by the aid of which the opposing impulses are built up, however much these tricks themselves may be the issue of our sense of values. Thus any impulses, any emotions, set up in excess of them, outside their orbit, so to speak, are not only useless lumber, but definite impediments to that peculiar settling of the nervous system, that 'full repose' at which tragedy aims. Thus, to use the image of Lisideius, we want to see the poet in sight of the goal, just upon us, and be free of 'the tedious expectation of seeing the poet set out and ride the beginning of the course'. For the human organization is too delicate to be tampered with; its agility and its power of assimilation are limited. This, again, is the argument for preserving the unity of place. It is not on account of its absurdity that it is a handicap to have 'Afrique of the one side, Asia of the other'; there is no difficulty in surrendering to that sort of illusion: but that it involves a readjustment of associations, a tapping of our mental energy. It is possible that to the average Jacobean playgoer Athens and Alexandria were just two names, which might as well have been Rome and Persepolis; but to us this is not so, and a change of place may in itself be unsettling beyond remedy.

One disadvantage of the panoramic method is at once clear; alone, it no more clarifies the emotions than the raw life. To make a tragedy out of North's History, we have ourselves to do the work of the tragedian; but the business of a playwright is not to give us the materials for a tragedy, but by the especial ordering of the materials to compel a peculiar balance. The amount of destructive material in *Antony and Cleopatra* is in consequence enormous. In construction alone—to leave out such considerations we are offered as to whether an eunuch has passions, or such additions as the 'ragging' of Lepidus on Pompey's ship— one need but point to the Actium scenes, or to that of Ventidius in Syria. The play is full of events which are not action. And here the question may pertinently be put: What do the first three acts of *Antony and Cleopatra* actually do towards ordering our emotions? This may perhaps best be answered by suggesting that it would not be at all incongruous for the play to end as a comedy, a result unthinkable at that stage in the plays of either

Daniel or Dryden. If these acts are unnecessary to the tragedy, they are obstructive, for time also is an important factor, since the tragic balance is not to be compelled all at once. Shakespeare was forced to contract all the tragic elements into the last two acts, and even the final speech of the play is marred because he still had something to tell us which he had found in North, namely that Cleopatra had experimented in poisons.

But before going on further to discuss the panoramic method, it may usefully be observed that to be able to keep to the unity of time in dealing with a complicated history implies a certain condition in the audience, for the form of a play is not entirely under the playwright's control. The condition is that the audience should previously know the story, if the tragic issue depends upon what has gone before. Daniel had the advantage of Shakespeare, one shared by Sophocles, Racine, and Dryden, and could plunge at once into the atmosphere of Cleopatra's ' monument '. Writing for the coterie which surrounded 'Sidney's sister, Pembroke's mother ', he could assume that his audience knew their Plutarch. Dryden could assume they knew their Shakespeare. Shakespeare himself had no such aid; he had to ride the beginning of the course before he could begin his real work. Given his material, the audience compelled the form.

The alternative to panoramic history is ' relation ', the telling of the tale, which has the disadvantage that it hangs up the action, a problem Ibsen was the first to solve. We suspend the flow of our emotions to consider history. There is, for instance, a dangerous moment in Act I of *The Tempest*, and in actual performance it is not always Miranda alone who is ' inclined to sleep '. But relation has this advantage—it allows of the full development of thought and comment. It involves, however, a much lower key if it is to be maintained, with the result that Daniel's play, which is almost entirely in relation (owing to his predilection for a certain form which was not thrust upon him), gives us ' rather a beautiful statue than a breather '. Nevertheless relation has its place, and can be extremely effective in short passages, especially if it bears, not on the event of the moment, but upon its emotions.

> He, at Philippi kept
> His sword e'en like a dancer, while I struck
> The lean and wrinkled Cassius.

This, Hazlitt says, ' is one of those fine retrospections which shows us the winding and eventful march of human life '. Then, in complete contradiction of the implications of his praise, he goes on to remark :

> The jealous attention which has been paid to the unities both of time and place has taken away the principle of perspective in the drama, and all the interest which objects derive from distance, from contrast, from privation, from change of fortune, from long-cherished passion ; and contracts our view of life from a strange, romantic dream, long, obscure, and infinite, into a smartly contested, three-hours' inaugural disputation on its merits by the different candidates for theatrical applause.

Apart from this strange conception of tragedy, Hazlitt, usually so brilliant, is here talking arrant nonsense. Dryden, working within the unities, can do precisely the same as Shakespeare, and on a larger scale than that of the passage Hazlitt quoted, the example which follows being chosen in preference to an available parallel :

> How I loved
> Witness ye days and nights, and all your hours
> That danced away with down upon your feet,
> As all your business were to count my passion.
> One day past by, and nothing saw but love ;
> Another came, and still 'twas only love : . . .

This advantage, then, of the panoramic method, seems to be without foundation; for what of retrospective do the first three acts of *Antony and Cleopatra* do that *All for Love* does not?

If it is right to assume that the effect of a drama is attained by movement of the emotions, it would appear that the panoramic method had one enormous advantage over the classical, for with each different scene—and there are thirty-eight in *Antony and Cleopatra*—a change in speed can at once be brought about. This is of prime value, and it might be possible to judge a play by its rhythmic structure alone. Yet to read *All for Love* immediately after *Antony and Cleopatra* is seriously to undermine one's opinion of the gain. For by Shakespeare's method there is room for only one emotion in each scene: the play proceeds by violent contrasts; the swaying back and forth of the emotions which will eventually lead to the 'full repose' (the term is Dryden's) is spasmodic. Shakespeare has to show Antony in a rage, or wild with jealousy, except when he speaks coldly, politically, and with thought which is not action, since it does nothing to develop character; his mind does not unfold itself as it does in *All for Love*: it is shown in a series of sharp disjuncted images, and therefore remains crude. On the other side, quite apart from the very definite and invariable emotive effects due to form alone, the keeping of each act entire allows for development of character, and a much subtler, surer, emotive progression. But of these things it is almost impossible to speak, because to substantiate the argument would need the quotation of a whole act from each play. Each act of *All for Love*, as Dryden claimed, concludes with a turn of the main design, not only of action, but of the emotion that leads to the action which is to complete it. Of the kind of thing here meant, the first scene between Antony and Cleopatra may be noted, though the illustration must be imperfect since it is fragmentary. Antony, having been won over by Ventidius, is being drawn back by Cleopatra, who is speaking:

How shall I plead my cause, when you my judge
Already have condemned me? Shall I bring
The love you bore me for my advocate?
That now is turned against me, that destroys me;
For, love once past, is, at the best, forgotten;
But oftener sours to hate: 'twill please my lord
To ruin me, and therefore I'll be guilty.
But, could I once have thought it would have pleased you,
That you would pry, with narrow, searching eyes
Into my faults, severe to my destruction,
And watching all advantages with care,
That serve to make me wretched? Speak, my lord,
For I end here. Though I deserve this usage,
Was it like you to give it?

It may with justice be argued that this is too life-like; that Shakespeare, with his intensification of reality, takes us out of the bounds of realism; that he has created a world which is not life, but like it; and that, unless we accept his premises we have not the right of entry into his realm. This is cogent; it is, indeed, the answer to Rymer on *Othello*: but for it to be valid the play needs to have a complete consistency, a rigorous exclusion of naturalism which Shakespeare did not achieve; nor could he, if he were to give nearly every 'event' mentioned by North. One has only to point to the scenes where Cleopatra receives the news of Antony's marriage to Octavia (II. 5 and III. 3) to illustrate the occasional lapse into complete realism. Shakespeare perhaps tried to avoid this, for often one feels that he is forcing the note to something beyond the natural; and this suggests another serious disadvantage in his method, which is, that to keep the drama interesting, the historical and merely 'eventful' part has to be heightened, so that the main actors in the drama seem to be in a passion equally high over indifferent things as over the significant actions. Take the first lines Antony and Cleopatra speak, not, it is true, over an indifferent thing, but at an insignificant moment:

Cleopatra. If it be love indeed, tell me how much.
Antony. There's beggary in the love that can be reckoned.
Cleopatra. I'll set a bourn how far to be beloved.
Antony. Then must thou needs find out new heav'n, new earth.

And this is not Nat Lee, but Shakespeare, who is, in this play, continually led into false rhetoric, such as:

Alexas. His speech sticks in my heart.
Cleopatra. Mine ear must pluck it thence.

or,

Cleopatra. Hence,
Horrible villain! or I'll spurn thine eyes
Like balls before me.

Diction.

At this point it is that one of the most important questions must be asked, which is: How far does form affect the diction and phrasing; and whether in this sphere the greater liberty of the panoramic form may not make up for its disadvantages? It would appear that form and phrasing are inextricably dependent upon one another. However, it is curious to note how Shakespeare is always 'classical' in the vivid imagery of his metaphor, whereas Daniel, with his vague suggestiveness, is much more 'romantic'; e. g. 'When that inexorable monster death', or purely intellectual, as in 'these summer swallows of felicity'. Perhaps, indeed probably, no rigid dividing line can be drawn between what is possible or impossible within the various forms, and the most that one can say is that one form favours one diction rather than another: at all events, in these three plays there are certain facts to be reckoned, and certain comparisons to be made.

Daniel's play is written in quatrains, but the occasional couplets often give the effect of complete sonnets in the Shakespearian manner. Dryden's is written in blank verse, ' in imitation of the divine Shakespeare ', but it is a verse very much less flexible than his original's, for in truth Dryden was incapable of that great and subtle variety of rhythm, of all those undertones and modulations which are the gift of Shakespeare alone. We must try to distinguish what is due to form, and what to difference in genius. But since in the classical way of writing it is essential to preserve a unity of tone, not a uniformity, but a change within definite limits, it would appear that to sustain this the poet must deny himself certain peaks, and, if not the more deeply searching phrases, the livelier extraneous pictures. He must certainly abjure the wilder flights of rhetoric. Shakespeare can afford to be splendidly rhetorical :

> Dissolve, thick cloud, and rain ; that I may say,
> The gods themselves do weep,

comes perfectly in *Antony and Cleopatra*, but would appear forced in *All for Love*. In the classical method all must be borne forward on an irresistible tide. Not that all Shakespeare's finest flashes would be inappropriate. The superb

> Peace, Peace !
> Dost not thou see my baby at my breast,
> That sucks the nurse asleep ?

might well have a place in *All for Love*, had not Dryden

studiously avoided taking anything of importance from
Shakespeare. Certainly if you can say with Dryden:

> When half the world fell mouldering from my hands,

you must admit Shakespeare's

> Finish, good lady; the bright day is done,
> And we are for the dark.

But the question arises, though you can say:

> What, to be led in triumph through the streets,
> A spectacle to base plebeian eyes;
> Whilst some dejected friend of Antony's
> Close in a corner, shakes his head and mutters
> A secret curse on her who ruined him?

is it possible to be as graphic as:

> Saucy lictors
> Will catch at us, like strumpets; and scald rhymers
> Ballad us out o' tune: the quick comedians
> Extemporally will stage us, and present
> Our Alexandrian revels. Antony
> Shall be brought drunken forth, and I shall see
> Some squeaking Cleopatra boy my greatness
> I' the posture of a whore.

Is that compatible with the classical form?

Let us now take a passage which shows the variance in
diction of the three methods, from which it would appear
that the formal method of relation slows down too much,
but that the panoramic method, with its naturalism forced
to rhetorical heights, brings about a diffusion. The scene
is described in North:

> But when they had opened the doors they found Cleopatra
> stark dead, laid upon a bed of gold, attired and arrayed in her
> royal robes, and one of her two women, which was called Iras,
> dead at her feet: and her other woman called Charmion half-
> dead, and trembling, trimming the diadem which Cleopatra ware
> upon her head. One of the soldiers seeing her, angrily said unto

her: 'Is that well done, Charmion?' 'Very well', said she again, 'and meet for a princess descended from the race of so many noble kings.' She said no more, but fell down dead hard by the bed.

DANIEL

For there they found, stretcht on a bed of gold,
Dead Cleopatra; and that proudly dead,
In all the rich attire procure she could;
And dying Charmion trimming of her head,
And Eras at her feet, dead in like case.
Charmion, is this well done? said one of them.
Yea, well, said she, and her that from the race
Of so great kings descends, doth best become.
And with that word, yields to her faithful breath,
To pass th' assurance of her love with death.

SHAKESPEARE

Iras had died after kissing Cleopatra, which elicits the terrible 'Have I the aspic in my lips?' When Cleopatra dies Charmian says:

> So, fare thee well.—
> Now boast thee, death, in thy possession lies
> A lass unparallel'd. Downy windows close,
> And golden Phœbus never be beheld
> Of eyes again so royal! Your crown's awry;
> I'll mend it, and then play.
> > *Enter Guards rushing in.*

First Gd.	Where is the queen?
Charmian.	Speak softly, wake her not.
First Gd.	Cæsar hath sent—
Charmian.	Too slow a messenger. (*Applies an asp.*)
	O! Come apace, despatch; I partly feel thee.
First Gd.	Approach, ho! All's not well: Cæsar's beguiled.
Second Gd.	There's Dolabella sent from Cæsar; call him.
First Gd.	What work is here!—Charmian, is this well done?
Charmian.	It is well done, and fitting for a princess
	Descended of so many royal kings.
	Ah, soldier! (*Dies.*)

DRYDEN

Cleopatra and Iras are dead; Antony dead beside Cleopatra.

Charmion stands behind the chair as dressing her head.   Enter Serapion, two priests, Alexas bound, Egyptians.

2nd *Priest.* Behold, Serapion, what havoc death has made.
Serapion. 'Twas what I feared.
        Charmion, is this well done?
Charmion. Yes, 'tis well done, and like a Queen, the last
        Of her great race. I follow her.

(Sinks down and dies.)

In Charmion's last speech it would seem that Dryden has the advantage, simply because of the more measured and restrained flow of his verse. Yet the passage from Daniel serves to show the advantage of relation, for the spoken word is often more impressive than the thing enacted before us. The beautiful line

And dying Charmion trimming of her head.

is merely a stage direction in Dryden. Shakespeare, feeling the need to supplement the action by words, put in ' Your crown's awry, I'll mend it, and then play'; but powerful as those plain words are after the flowery passage, it is doubtful if they are as emotive as Daniel's.

In his *Defence of Rhyme* Daniel remarked of it that ' in an eminent spirit, whom nature hath fitted for that mystery, rhyme is no impediment to his conceit, but rather gives him wings to mount, and carries him, not out of his course, but as it were beyond his power to a far happier flight', a conclusion M. Paul Valéry has also reached: ' elle y appelle de très loin une multitude de pensées qui ne s'attendaient pas d'être conçues'.* Certainly, for its effect on the listener, in ordering the impulses to one end, it is very valuable; but it may be doubted if Daniel's argument is

* *Variété*, p. 61.   19th Edition.

applicable to the stage, the more so when we remember that Dryden's argument was the exact reverse (see p. 46). But the latter was speaking of the couplet, which, as he used it, does indeed have the effect he states; for even in *Aureng-Zebe*, his freest attempt, the grammatical unit seldom overflows the couplet. But though abandoning rhyme for this play, he tightened up blank verse, which had run to seed in Shakespeare's successors. In so doing he definitely denied himself the broader rhythm, the wider sweep: but Daniel, in using the quatrain, surely gave himself too large a unit, which too much slows down and distends the thought:

> When yet we reckon life our dearest good.
> And so we live, we care not how we live :
> So deep we feel impressed in our blood
> That touch which nature with our * breath did give —
> And yet what blasts of words hath learning found
> To blow against the fear of death and dying. . .

and he takes eighteen more lines to exhaust the idea. Dryden is pithy, and accomplishes in four lines the same thing it took Daniel twenty to do:

> O that I less could fear to lose this being,
> Which, like a snowball in my coward hand,
> The more 'tis grasped, the faster melts away.
> Poor reason ! what a wretched aid art thou !
> For still, in spite of thee,
> These two long lovers, soul and body, dread
> Their final separation.

Whatever the demerits of the couplet may be, it is evidently splendid training for writing blank verse.

To compare, however, the two methods, not only of versification, we may take a passage Daniel had no chance to use.

* Grosart's edition has 'without'. I owe the emendation to a critic of The Times Literary Supplement.

NORTH

I am sorry that, having been so great a captain and emperor, I am indeed condemned to be judged of less courage and noble mind than a woman. .. O noble Eros, I thank thee for this, and it is valiantly done of thee, to show me what I should do to myself, which thou could'st not do for me.

SHAKESPEARE

                    Since Cleopatra died,
I have lived in such dishonour, that the gods
Detest my baseness. I, that with my sword
Quartered the world, and o'er green Neptune's back
With ships made cities, condemn myself to lack
The courage of a woman: less noble mind
Than she, which by her death our Cæsar tells
'I am conqueror of myself.'

(Some forty lines follow, at the end of which Eros kills himself.)

                    Thrice nobler than myself!
Thou teachest me, O valiant Eros, what
I should, and thou could'st not. My Queen and Eros
Have by their brave instruction got upon me
A nobleness in record; but I will be
A bridegroom in my death, and run into't
As to a lover's bed.

DRYDEN

So Antony, after Ventidius had killed himself:

Farewell! Ever my leader, even in death!
My queen and thou have got the start of me;
And I'm the lag of honour.

But if Dryden is here again magnificently condensed, the advantage is not always with the more restrained form; and here is an example where the naturalistic method seems to gain over the others. The idea is not in North, but it is in Daniel, where Nuntius relates:

Well, in I went, where brighter than the sun,
Glittering in all her pompeous rich array,

> Great Cleopatra sat, as if sh'had won
> Cæsar, and all the world beside, this day :
> Even as she was when on thy crystal streams
> Clear Cydnos, she did show what earth could show;
> When Asia all amazed in wonder, deems
> Venus from heaven was come on earth below.
> Even as she went at first to meet her love,
> So goes she now again to find him.
> But that first, did her greatness only prove,
> This last her love, that could not live behind him.

Dryden, in strict conformity with the tone of the whole act, has :

Charmion. To what end
These ensigns of your pomp and royalty?
Cleopatra. Dull that thou art ! why, 'tis to meet my love ;
As when I saw him first, on Cydno's bank
All sparkling, like a goddess ; so adorned
I'll find him once again. My second spousals
Shall match my first, in glory. Haste, haste, both,
And dress the bride of Antony.

But this is Shakespeare :

> Show me, my women, like a queen : go fetch
> My best attires ; I am again for Cydnus,
> To meet Mark Antony.

There is no doubt there which is the most dramatic and pithy, and therefore the most poetic.

Shakespeare's fancy is not one to wish bounded and circumscribed, though we are sometimes glad, in Dryden, to be rid of the earlier floweriness, and references to pagan gods. Nevertheless Shakespeare's verse sometimes ran away with him : the following passage is magnificent, but would it not be better without the last line, which is something of an example of sinking?

> For his bounty,
> There was no winter in't; an autumn 'twas
> That grew the more by reaping : his delights

> Were Dolphin-like; they showed his back above
> The element they lived in: in his livery
> Walked crowns and crownets; realms and islands were
> As plates dropped from his pocket.

The whole speech with its beginning, 'His legs bestrid the Ocean,' is a superb piece of rhetoric, far outdistancing even Dryden's

> We two have kept its homage in suspense,
> And bent the globe on whose each side we troa
> Till it was dented inwards,

(The parallel passage in Shakespeare is 'We could not stall together in the whole world'.) Whether a stricter manner of writing would have caused Shakespeare to have blotted his last line is doubtful, but it would certainly have prevented him from writing such a line as

> And hoist thee up to the shouting plebeians.

But if the classical method may save from false, it prevents the rise to the heights of right rhetoric, that summit of the dramatists' art; and Dryden, where he makes Antony compare himself with Mars, is perilously near bombast. Nevertheless he can rise very high:

> O horror, horror!
> Egypt has been: our latest hour is come:
> The Queen of nations from her ancient seat
> Is sunk for ever in the dark abyss:
> Time has unrolled her glories to the last
> And now closed up the volume.

Yet it seems to lack the larger rhythm; the influence of the couplet is here too circumscribing: apart from the question of actual thought, the manner would hardly admit:

> O! see, my women,
> The crown o' the earth doth melt. My lord!
> O! withered is the garland of the war,
> The soldier's pole is fallen: young boys and girls

> Are level now with men; the odds is gone,
> And there is nothing left remarkable
> Beneath the visiting moon.

It is, perhaps, not altogether fair to divorce a passage from its context, for the setting counts for much, and this consideration must modify any conclusion to be drawn from parallels. Almost the same words may have quite a different effect when variously placed, how much so may be seen from a phrase of Shakespeare's Antony already quoted here, and one of Claudio's in *Measure for Measure*:

> I will encounter darkness as a bride
> And hug it in my arms.

The comparison of the two famous passages, born of North, describing Cleopatra on Cydnus has here been avoided, for Shakespeare and Dryden were not at all at the same thing. With the latter the passage is a tender reminiscence of Antony's; with Shakespeare it is Enobarbus at once burlesquing Antony's feeling for Cleopatra, and trying to *épater le bourgeois* in Mæcenas and Agrippa. This at any rate is a plausible supposition, when we consider that Enobarbus, a thoughtful character, never loses a chance of gibing at Cleopatra, that he goes on to describe a lack of breath as a virtue in almost the same terms as Pandarus uses to praise Cressida, and that he ends up

> for vilest things
> Become themselves in her, that the holy priests
> Bless her when she is riggish.

The doubt of Shakespeare's intentions disappears on carefully reading the whole passage, with its ' Antony being barbered ten times o'er ' setting the whole tone of it. It is difficult to believe it was meant as anything but a satirical flight, in spite of all the imperishable phrases it contains.

Final Effects.

Rémy de Gourmont remarked that 'Un livre que la vénération des siècles a sacré n'est plus un livre ; c'est une partie de la nature,' that is, it is extremely hard to separate it from our associations. But if the effect of tragedy is, after adventuring, to produce free contemplation, detached from personal fears and desires, disilluded, it would seem, from nearly all the critics who have written of it, that Shakespeare's play fails of this effect. There is hardly one who has not been left in love with Cleopatra, feeling that life is rich and exciting, who is not, in sum, swayed by the emotions a gorgeous story provokes. The proof that they are beglamoured lies in their very panegyrics upon Cleopatra. Grave and reverend signors declare her to be the flower of womanhood, the *ewige weibliche*, as Leda, the mother of Helen of Troy, and, as Saint Anne, the mother of Mary. This is a strange conception, due, perhaps, to that very English desire, the other side of the puritan medal, to find in imagination a woman to whom they could physically and morally abandon themselves, though in reality they might flee from her arms to those of the mother of the Gracchi. For turn what Shakespeare says into the prose of the daily paper, see the object as it really is, and she appears as vulgar as Plutarch makes her, fit indeed for a gaudy night, but preposterous, superficial, cruel, and greedy, of the flesh fleshy, with intelligence only enough to make a pun upon the name Toryne, to practise the seductive arts of a low-born trollop, and cause salted fish to be placed on Antony's hook, treatments, by the way, he richly deserved. Not a man of these critics but would be Antony if he could ; but who would be Œdipus, Phedre, or Lear ?

It may be said that all the foregoing observations are beside the point, since the object of Shakespeare was not that of Daniel or of Dryden. These last were aiming at the production of a certain effect by selecting their elements, and expressing them in an especial economy. Dryden, to set aside Daniel's less dramatic poem, undoubtedly achieves sustained beauty. He had, to use an expression of Landor's, this of godlike in him, a love of order, and the power of bringing great things into it. Shakespeare seems to be aiming at something which comes from below the sense of, or the desire for, beauty : his work is informed by a more inclusive feeling. After reading *All for Love* we are conscious of having heard glorious music : after reading *Antony and Cleopatra*, the voices of men and women, the clash of events, resound in our ears, and the music is but an incidental, if pervading element. Indeed, in one sense, Shakespeare shows himself more classical than Dryden, for the latter is concerned with emotions rather than with facts : at least it is through the statements of emotions rather than through vision of facts, that he gets his effects, a method which resembles Shakespeare's in *Measure for Measure*.

But to whatever extent doubt may overcast the possible conclusions here suggested, one thing is certain : the classical method rigorously excluded comic relief. Not necessarily humour, as Ventidius's apt and admirable speech to Alexas is enough to show :

> There's news for you : run, my officious eunuch,
> Be sure to be the first ; haste forward :
> Haste, my dear eunuch, haste.

Yet it definitely cuts out that use of the comic to throw into high light the agony of terrible events, a relief Shakespeare used to the full in the scene where the 'clown' brings Cleopatra the asps. The danger of such relief is that it may harrow too much, that the subtle structure of appetencies and satisfactions may be deranged. Our emotions may be disordered so as to seek relief, in the other sense of the word, by hysterical laughter or a sob, and this is not the end of tragedy. The clown scene is indeed strong meat to digest into any ordered system, and it is questionable whether the general tone of Shakespeare's play will bear it, as *Lear* bears similar scenes. It would certainly destroy *All for Love*. Yet such contrasts, if successful, probe more deeply than anything common in the classical method. Think, in Shakespeare, of Antony's twice repeated ' I'm dying, Egypt, dying,' flung against Cleopatra's wild, egotistical, almost ' low ' babble. The phrase comes with terrible effect ; it is a tremendous summation ; but its simplicity, its grandeur, would be lost in the general grandeur of *All for Love*. It would come greatly anywhere, but not with that supreme force with which Shakespeare invests it.

In the main, it is Shakespeare's poetic genius in the use of metaphor, his incomparable capacity for marrying ideas, his irresistible mind working ever on the word and making it flesh, which makes his play more universal than Dryden's. It is chock full of unforgettable things—her barge burned on the water—corrigible neck—like a doting mallard—rivetted trim—I have immortal longings in me : the play would furnish forth half a dozen *All for Loves*, good poet though Dryden be. Dryden, in the use of the lambent phrase, the metaphor that vanquishes or seduces, in the revealing word that lightens like a flash, is far below Shakespeare, Webster, or Tourneur. It may be that he is too given to the simile rather than the metaphor, though he does not in this play much indulge in those portentous paragraphs ushered in with ' As when . . . ' which Fielding made such delicious fun of in *Tom Thumb the Great*. As a poet he is not on the same ground with Marlowe; though his country may be as beautiful; he could never have written

> See, see, where Christ's blood streams in the firmament.

Yet, in its result, *All for Love* is more decisively a tragedy than any of those above referred to except Shakespeare's best, and *Antony and Cleopatra* is not one of them. Many plays of the earlier period contain finer things than Dryden ever wrote, but as wholes they are patchy. Their makers were never certain within what limits they worked, or they defiantly flouted the limits, like Webster, who declared, ' willingly, and not ignorantly, in this kind have I faulted '. Thus their works are not in their final effect so near tragedy as Dryden's masterpiece. The barriers of form justify themselves in actual practice, for the frame of those plays is too diffuse, containing too many emotional values, in number beyond the power of ordering. Dryden's play has a coherence, a direction to one end, in a word, a unity, which we may wrest from the others, but which they do not, like his, compel.

V

JOHN DRYDEN (1631—1700) AND ARTIFICIAL TRAGEDY

The Indian Emperor, 1665.
Tyrranick Love, 1669.
The Conquest of Granada, 1670.
Amboyna, 1673.
Aureng-Zebe, 1675.
All for Love, 1677.
Don Sebastian, 1689.
Cleomenes, 1692.

It is curious that the word ' artificial ' should for more than a century have been applied to the most realistic comedy written in this country; for Restoration comedy, far from being as artificial as that of Aristophanes, of Shakespeare in, say *Love's Labour's Lost*, of Molière, Wilde, or Mr. Shaw, is much closer to everyday life, both in detail and in mental reaction, than any of those mentioned. On the other hand, the epithet can most happily be applied to the tragedy of the age, for there the emotions were deliberately invented. *Lear* is not artificial because the feelings are real; they are not so in most heroic tragedy.

' Artificial ' should not be used as a term of abuse, since it is largely the artificiality which makes a work permanent: a piece of literature needs, to pass muster, only enough of reality to make it understandable. Restoration tragedy was real enough, if not in experience, at least in desire, to make it appeal. It mapped out, not the actualities of human emotion, but its ideals; which was unfortunate for itself, since, while feelings remain unchanged, ideals are various. Moreover, it works out in practice that where ideals are the material, only form can make a work last. But indeed, any tragedy which deals with the fundamental ethical problem of life, the question of good and evil, is in a sense artificial, the difference between a good tragedy and a bad one consisting mainly in how far the problem is passionate or intellectual; it is the difference between *Macbeth* and *Cato*. But the artificiality here meant is something more obvious; and what as much as anything else betrays the weakness of Restoration tragedy is that the artificiality soon degenerated into the sentimental. The sentimental is that which takes the immaterial to be the real (using the words in their most evident sense), and ascribes more importance to the feeling, than to the fact which is supposed to arouse the feeling. As Sterne realized, to blubber over a dead donkey as though he were your brother, is sentimental. Thus sentimentality is only another name for falsity. Where it occurs there is no correspondence, taking the generality of human feeling as the norm, between emotion and fact: the first is not of necessity in excess of the second, it is beside it.

It turns out then, that where the content is not based upon experience, it is form alone which can make an object: and always when reading Dryden, it strikes one that he wrote, not to portray feeling, except in *All for Love* and some scattered scenes, but to make a thing. Again and again, as we have seen, he pointed out the distinction between art and life. And form in a play is not, as even nineteenth-century doctrine would have it, so much one of plot, of structure of scenes, as of structure of emotions played off against each other. What is dramatic is not tension, but change of tension. Given but a limited range of reality in emotion, and by careful structure a delightful object can be made. This is what Dryden could do supremely: in spite of the unreality of the feelings, his things last by the sheer force of their artificiality. Clearly it is idle to blame Dryden for not painting the passions, since that was not what he was trying to do.

Yet he is never sentimental, for there was too much common sense in Dryden, too much respect for judgement as opposed to fancy, to allow him to divorce himself entirely from reality, and be 'heaven-born' after the manner of Settle. Thus in the Postscript to the *Notes and Observations on the Empress of Morocco* he wrote:

> Mere poets and mere musicians are as sottish as mere drunkards are, who live in a continual mist, without seeing or judging anything clearly.
>
> A man should be learned in several sciences, and should have a reasonable, philosophical, and in some measure a mathematical head, to be a complete and excellent poet ; and besides this, should have experience in all sorts of humours and manners of men, should be thoroughly skilled in conversation, and should have a great knowledge of mankind in general.

Learned in several sciences Dryden certainly was not : but by virtue of being thoroughly skilled in conversation, he was in touch with all the currents of thought of his day. If he had not read Hobbes carefully, he knew what Hobbes was about, and shared his political views, so much so as to make them part and parcel of the 'character' of some of his persons. He was abreast of the new science of his time, as far as a layman may be, and if his method of argument was often medieval, his attitude towards the thing argued was essentially modern. If he had no consistent scheme of philosophy, he had enough knowledge of it for metaphor ; and indeed, enough familiarity with the world of thought as well as that of action, to enable him to strike out those bold generalizations which stick in the mind, and in themselves give a partial permanence to drama. Without such generalizations, 'moral sentences' as Dryden called them,

no drama can live ; the popular quotations from Shakespeare
are nearly all maxims or aphorisms, where they are not
descriptions which might as well occur in lyrical or narrative
poems as in a play.

Indeed, if we seek in Dryden some definite message, or
some especial attitude, we shall seek in vain. If this is a
defect in him, it is one which he shares with Shakespeare.
All that we can feel for certain in considering the two, is
a difference in the wholeness of their attitudes; we know
that though both of them approached life in a multitude of
ways, they approached it at different levels. We may suggest
the difference roughly by saying that Shakespeare was meta-
physical where Dryden was moral. It is true that here and
there Dryden would appear to have been aiming at ultimate
values, concluding, however, rather negatively, in such
things as the famous

> When I consider life, 'tis all a cheat ;
> Yet, fooled with hope, men favour the deceit :
> Trust on, and think to-morrow will repay ;
> To-morrow's falser than the former day ;
> Lies worse ; and while it says, we shall be blest
> With some new joys, cuts off what we possest.
> Strange cozenage ! none would live past years again,
> Yet all hope pleasure in what yet remain ;
> And, from the dregs of life, think to receive
> What the first sprightly running could not give.
> I'm tired with waiting for this chymick gold,
> Which fools us young, and beggars us when old.
>
>   (*Aureng-Zebe*, IV. i.)

One is even tempted to believe that this state of mind was
common with him, gave a permanent colouring to his life,
since he repeated it so often. One is the more inclined to
do so, as his is one of the first, though not the very first
statement in English literature, of the consciousness of
thought as a vital disease, a consciousness which can only

have emerged in an age when thought, instead of being used to bolster up faith, was being used to inquire into and undermine it. It is now a commonplace; we meet it for instance in Keats, 'Where but to think is to be full of sorrow', or in

> It is a flaw
> In happiness to see beyond our bourne,—
> It forces us in summer skies to mourn,
> It spoils the singing of the nightingale.

But there is no proof, far the contrary in fact, that such a feeling was permanent in Dryden : that he should have expessed it again and again is only another illustration of Dr. Johnson's remarks that he never lacked words to clothe his thoughts, and that his fancy never languished for penury of ideas. A thought which had once occurred to him as useful for his dramatic purposes might easily occur again, and would naturally appear in fresh words. Take the same sentiment as expressed by Almahide, in *The Conquest of Granada* (II. I. ii):

> Man only clogs with cares his happiness :
> And, while he should enjoy his part of bliss,
> With thoughts of what may be, destroys what is.

Or differently again in *The Indian Queen* (III. i):

> Grief seldom joined with blooming youth is seen,
> Can sorrow be where knowledge scarce has been ?
> Fortune does well for heedless youth provide,
> But wisdom does unlucky age misguide.

In the same way other themes are continually cropping up in his plays; such as the iniquity of a subject criticizing his monarch; his cynicism as regards priests of all denominations; or a general religious scepticism. No especial thought, then, seems to attach to him : it is only that in attaching the thoughts of others to himself he made them, for the time being at least, indubitably his own.

His material being just what thoughts he could lay his hands on,—the philosophies, so far as he entered into them, of his day, the actions and tumults of the age—the point of interest with him is to try to see what he made of them, what sort of object he managed to create. No one can deny that Dryden's plays give delight; if not all of them give pleasure completely in their wholeness as well as in their detail, none of them lacks passages which are sure to be enjoyed. And the quality which emerges is *prettiness*; his classicism does not produce austerity, but, as in certain architectural returns to the classics, the graces, the unexpected charms, the will to astonish agreeably, of the *baroque*. Nor is it forcing the metaphor too far to say that much of the pleasure derived from his work is a sense of the architectural, totally absent from, say, the later work of Otway. Indeed, Dryden's triumph is only obvious if we insist upon this prettiness, for that sort of quality is only bearable where a hard structure is there to support it. He had the root of the matter in him, the ability to use the hard stone, the solid masses; and the prettiness is twofold, existing in the arrangement of the main blocks as well as in the decoration; nor is it ever a mere prettiness of sentiment, such as occasionally appears in Otway, marring his work. Indeed, it has long been notorious that Dryden was by no means at his best in the ' tender ' passages; he failed to do for love what he could do so splendidly for masculine friendship. It is commonplace that it is not to the love scenes, even in *All for Love*, that one goes for his best expression of emotion, but to the scene of the reconciliation of Antony and Ventidius in that play, or of Sebastian and Alonzo in *Don Sebastian*. His prettiness is not accidental; it is the result of labour; it is the sheer artificiality of his plays which gives them their high place.

To make good the claim of grace of structure is impossible without quotation of a whole act, a difficulty that we have met with before: the most that can be done is to explain what is meant by this, and to appeal to the reader's experience of Dryden, or ask him to go back to him. Thus it must now be more emphatically stated that what finally is meant by structure is the sequence of emotions in the hearer; and that good structure is where the emotions are well woven, appropriately opposed, and conducted to some definite end. With Dryden the end is never a terrific emotion, a frozen staring at fate or fortune, a fatalistic acceptance of life, such as we feel at the conclusion of the greatest tragedies, *Othello*, say, or *Œdipus Rex*. It is, rather, a graciousness, a compensation for the hardness of existence, that we are led to feel, such graciousness as is not altogether absent from classical tragedy, as in the *Œdipus at Colonus*. How exactly it is that the emotions are aroused, checked, made to play upon one another, our learned doctors have not yet discovered; a writer can only guess at the secret by searching in his own experience, and it is enough to clear Dryden of the charge of having no feeling to point to his amazing success in bringing the result about. Amazing, but not unerring, for he often lapsed into too flamboyant a heroism, or sunk to too ready a matter-of-factness. Yet, in the main, he achieved what he wished: and if at the end we do not feel as we do after a tragedy of Sophocles, Shakespeare, or Racine, it is because he did not attempt to make us do so. He definitely tried to build up something different from life. And it is here that structure in the sense defined is relevant, for it is the proportion of the emotions, the varied strength of their impact, the general impression of their relation to one another, that determines the kind of balance finally attained. And in Dryden's plays the general impression of their relation is one of grace, or, to return to the word used above, of prettiness.

Prettiness is not a derogatory term; it is a quality which distinguishes Spenser and Marvell from lesser poets. And though it is not an epithet to be applied to Milton, the quality is not absent from Shakespeare, as, for example, in the last scene of *Measure for Measure*, or in much of *Twelfth Night*, to choose out of a score of instances. On the other hand, it is entirely absent from Webster, Tourneur, or Marston; and if it exists in Fletcher, it is there too sugary to give satisfaction, since it depends on sentiment, sweetness of phrasing, or the happy issue of the fable. With Dryden it is inseparable from the arrangement, and the feeling remains even when the play ends in woe. Take, for instance, the passage near the end of *Don Sebastian*, where the horror-stricken hero discovers that he has married his sister, keeping in mind that a short extract can only roughly adumbrate a process which gains its force owing to its operation throughout a play.

> *Seb.* To expiate this, can I do more than die?
> *Dor.* O yes, you must do more, you must be damn'd
> You must be damn'd to all eternity;
> And sure self-murder is the readiest way.
> *Seb.* How, damn'd?
> *Dor.* Why, is that news?
> *Alv.* O horror, horror!
> *Dor.* What, thou a statesman,
> And make a business of damnation
> In such a world as this! Why, 'tis a trade;
> The scrivener, usurer, lawyer, shopkeeper,
> And soldier, cannot live but by damnation.
> The politician does it in advance,
> And gives all gone beforehand.
> *Seb.* O thou hast given me such a glimpse of hell,
> So pushed me forward, even to the brink
> Of that irremeable burning gulph,

That, looking in the abyss, I dare not leap.
And now I see what good thou mean'st my soul,
And thank thy pious fraud; thou hast indeed
Appeared a devil, but did'st an angel's work.

Dor. 'Twas the last remedy, to give you leisure;
For, if you would but think, I knew you safe.

Seb. I, thank thee, my Alonzo; I will live,
But never more to Portugal return;
For to go back and reign, that were to show
Triumphant incest, and pollute the throne.

Alv. Since ignorance——

Seb. O, palliate not my wound;
When you have argued all you can, 'tis incest.
No, 'tis resolved: I charge you plead no more;
I cannot live without Almeyda's sight,
Nor can I see Almeyda, but I sin.
Heaven has inspired me with a sacred thought,
To live alone to heaven, and die to her.

Dor. Mean you to turn an anchorite?

Seb. What else?
The world was once too narrow for my mind,
But one poor little nook will serve me now,
To hide me from the rest of human kind.
Afric has deserts wide enough to hold
Millions of monsters; and I am, sure, the greatest.

Alv. You may repent, and wish your crown too late.

Seb. O never, never; I am past a boy:
A sceptre's but a plaything, and a globe
A bigger bounding stone. He, who can leave
Almeyda, may renounce the rest with ease.

Dor. O truly great!
A soul fix'd high, and capable of heaven.
Old as he is, your uncle cardinal
Is not so far enamour'd of a cloister,
But he will thank you for the crown you leave him.

Seb. To please him more, let him believe me dead,
That he may never dream I may return.
Alonzo, I am now no more thy king,
But still thy friend; and by that holy name
Adjure thee, to perform my last request;——
Make our conditions with yon captive king;
Secure me but my solitary cell;

> 'Tis all I ask him for a crown restored.
>
> *Dor.* I will do more :
> But fear not Muley Zeydan ; his soft metal
> Melts down with easy warmth, runs in the mould,
> And needs no further forge.

It cannot, of course, be maintained that the result is achieved without the unfailing charm of sound with which Dryden could, and did, fill his verse brimful. Even the ' irremeable burning gulph ' is robbed of its horrors, for by reason of the music it is not so acutely seen as to bring it out of the artificial picture. In the sort of thing Dryden was doing, it is a virtue; to have shuddered with the cardinal in *The Duchess of Malfi* :

> When I look into the fish-ponds in my garden,
> Methinks I see a thing armed with a rake,
> That seems to strike at me,

would have been too gruesome, just as for Webster's cardinal to have declaimed Sebastian's lines would have been too weak. For though Dryden was at times a master of structure, in the modern cant sense, he was first and foremost an artificer of words, in the way that Tennyson was. Tennyson continually reminds one of Dryden. Such lines as

> So sleeping, so aroused from sleep
> Thro' sunny decads new and strange,
> Or gay quinquenniads would we reap
> The flower and quintessence of change,

at once throw us back to the older poet. The theme is different, the measure more important in the passage quoted above, than in this which follows from *Aureng-Zebe*, but the appeal is the same, an irresistible prettiness of sound :

> Speak, Madam, by (if that be yet an oath)
> Your love, I'm pleased we should be ruined both.

> Both is a sound of joy.
> In death's dark bow'rs our bridals we will keep:
> And his cold hands
> Shall draw the curtain when we go to sleep.

Artificiality can go no further than that; but precisely because the sentiments are not brought into the stark light either of realism or of tragic reality, they never become sentimental.

There is much to say about Dryden.; but since nearly all, if not quite all (for something must always remain over with so great a man) has been said by abler pens, only one or two points will be expanded here. It is not the purpose of this chapter to expatiate upon his power, his command of rise and fall in verse, his tremendous energy—that quality of the first importance, as Landor insisted; nor is it necessary to observe his lapses, the occasional places where he undoubtedly became ridiculous, erring with his time, as in the fantastic wickedness of his villains, the *reductio ad absurdum*, as it is the relic, of the Elizabethan 'Machiavellism'. Yet, in this connexion, it is worth while to point out that much which appears forced and strained when read in the study, will pass amid the hurry and the clang of the stage, especially in the tremendous blare and colour of the Restoration theatre, where, as Addison complained, the distance from the hero's chin to the top of his plume, was greater than that from his neck to his feet. What will be stressed here, besides the quality of prettiness already dealt with, is the interest he produces by the strength of his words, and the charm he achieves by the grace of his manner.

Credit for much of the charm must be given to the delightfulness of his songs: bating the famous odes, there is nowhere that Dryden shows his lyrical quality so well as in these. Moreover, to look at a collection of them is to be struck by his astonishing variety in this form, his freedom among all kinds of styles and metres. But the moment one begins to notice his power of song-making, one becomes aware of the lyrical element which runs through the whole of his dramatic work, not only in the definitely operatic pieces, or in the *Secular Masque*, but in the more formal tragedies. Disquisitions which may be called philosophic, or even theological, have something of this quality, just as really it is a kind of lyricism in structure which distinguishes his plays from those of his contemporaries. Let us glance for a moment at *The Indian Emperor*, written in 1665, and thus one of his earliest plays. In many ways it best represents his praiseworthy artificiality, and is completely successful in what it tries to do. It has not the sonority, nor the power, of *All for Love*, or *Don Sebastian*; it has not that concentration of meaning in a phrase that he could get in his later work. There is nothing, for instance, to compare with the strong recitative passages of *Albion and Albianus*, such as:

> One, who has gained a body fit for sin;
> Where all his crimes
> Of former times
> Lie crowded in a skin,

where apart from the fact that satire sharpens the pen, Dryden had reached the point where he could make a line hold twice as much as he could before. Yet there is definitely something besides the dramatic appropriateness of the speeches, or the obvious meaning of the words, which makes the lines exist for themselves.

> I'll seize thee there, thou messenger of fate:
> Would my short life had yet a shorter date!

> I'm weary of this flesh which holds us here,
> And dastards manly souls with hope and fear;
> These heats and colds still on our breasts make war,
> Agues and fevers all our passions are.   (II. i.)

Or, still on the same theme:

> In wishing nothing, we enjoy still most;
> For even our wish is, in possession, lost:
> Restless we wander to a new desire,
> And burn ourselves by blowing up the fire:
> We toss and turn about our feverish will,
> When all our ease must come by lying still:
> For all the happiness mankind can gain
> Is not in pleasure, but in rest from pain.   (IV. i.)

Or, as expressing religious scepticisms:

> In seeking happiness you both agree;
> But in the search, the paths so different be,
> That all religions with each other fight,
> While only one can lead us in the right.
> But till that one hath some more certain mark,
> Poor human kind must wander in the dark.   (V. ii.)

However, a speech in a play cannot be completely lyrical: it hangs too much upon what has immediately gone before, and what is to come after: it cannot afford to be purposeless enough. Dryden seems to have felt exactly how far a speech could be lyrical without standing too much out of its context, a knowledge by no means shared by the Elizabethans, even by Shakespeare. None of the three quoted above are self-existent: yet each is distinct enough to show up as a facet in a jewel of complicated cut. Dryden's plays are largely built up of such things set together; they are the blocks, as it were, of which his architectural masses are composed. Perhaps it was necessary for there to be something of a singing quality about the parts, since most of his work does not depend for its force upon the onrush of events as the greatest tragedies do. Thus when he came

really to write a song, it had all the more to become independent, to detach itself by virtue of its completeness in
form, especially if the general tone was to be maintained.
Thus, in the same play:

> Ah fading joy! how quickly art thou past!
>   Yet we thy ruin haste:
> As if the cares of human life were few,
>   We seek out new,
> And follow fate that does too fast pursue.
>
> See how on ev'ry bough the birds express,
>   In their sweet notes, their happiness.
>   They all enjoy, and nothing spare;
> But on their mother Nature lay their care:
> Why then should man, the lord of all below,
>   Such troubles choose to know,
> As none of all his subjects undergo?
>
> Hark, hark, the waters fall, fall, fall,
> And with a murmuring sound
> Dash, dash, upon the ground,
>   To gentle slumbers call.

That song, evidently, is in line with the general feeling of
the piece, yet is perfect in itself. And, moreover, Dryden
knew where to place his songs, just so as to introduce the
change of emotion, or the change in the speed of the action
which itself produces emotion, to get the effect he wanted.

It may justly be argued that this form of play may well
lead to mere bric-a-brac of literature, just as the *baroque* in
building may lead to a bric-a-brac form of architecture.
But, after all, it is wholly a question of the judgement
controlling the fancy, especially in the use of materials.
The passions in Dryden may not be profoundly real, but
they are real enough to be serious. And this reality is
evoked purely out of the use of the word, which is the
essence of poetry as much as the rhythm or the image;
and the older Dryden grew, the stronger his power over

words became. Indeed, his object in life was to put words
to their utmost use, to refine the language, to cast out
barbarisms, preserve old words worth preserving, and to
import new ones from abroad, all in the interests of vigour
and lucidity. Thus, in the Preface to *Don Sebastian* he
drew attention in the play to 'some newness of English,
translated from the beauties of modern tongues, as well as
from the elegancies of the Latin; and here and there some
old words are sprinkled, which, for their significance and
sound, deserved not to be antiquated'. He had no need to
cudgel his brains to find thoughts in plenty; they crowded
fast upon him, as he said. They were not original thoughts;
they were rarely profound, but they were wide in their
range, and as deep as any that occur in plays except in
the works of the great masters. But with most writers who
are not original, the thoughts do not seem true, because
they do not clothe themselves with their proper words at
birth; one knows that some one has draped them. Dryden,
however, by his genius for the word, could give the thoughts
he found the same vividness as those have which appeal to
a writer as being true because they have come to birth
within him. That is why he was so admirable a translator,
and why some of the most admired passages in his plays
are direct from the Latin. His artistry is most apparent in
that he never tried to make his words or his form carry
anything weightier than they could bear. Thus it is absurd
to belittle his rhymed, operatic version of *Paradise Lost*.
Given the form of the verse which he was endeavouring
his best to make perfect, given the sort of play in which
he found himself most at ease, it would have been fatal to
aim at the solid grandeur of Milton's poem. Read *The
State of Innocence* (1677) without thinking of the source, and
it is a delightful thing. *All for Love* will stand comparison

with Shakespeare's play because it is meant to: Dryden's *Troilus and Cressida* and *The Tempest* will not stand such comparison with the originals because they are falsifications, though it is unnecessary to say that they are full of delicious corners. But there is no platform upon which *Paradise Lost* and *The State of Innocence* can be judged together. Look, for instance, at the 'vision', that interlude of sheer Restoration comedy, written in a lilting measure:

> Now wider experience has taught you to prove,
> What a folly it is,
> Out of fear to shun bliss.
> To the joy that's forbidden we eagerly move ;
> It enhances the price, and increases the love:

where, however, the strength of the word is as apparent as in the more famous

> Is all the sad variety of hell.

But it is, naturally, to his later work that we must turn for the full development of his powers in this respect. *Cleomenes* (1692) was his last pure tragedy, which, though not within reach of his finest work, owes hardly anything to prettiness of ornament, except for a few rhymed passages, but all to structure, movement, and especially to apt phrasing. There are no heights of rhetoric, no markedly sonorous passages, but it lives—or at least is very readable—simply because the best word is used in every place.

> *Pantheus.* All closed ; nothing but heaven above is open.
> *Cleomenes.* Nay, that's closed too ; the gods are deaf to prayers!
> Hush then ; th' irrevocable doom's gone forth,
> And prayers lag after, but can ne'er o'ertake—
> Let us talk forward of our woes to come.
> *Cratesiclea.* Cleanthes! (Oh, could you suspect his faith ?)
> 'Twas he, that headed those, who forced her hence.
> *Cleomenes.* Pantheus bleeds!
> *Pantheus.* A scratch, a feeble dart,
> At distance thrown by an Egyptian hand.

Cratesiclea.   You heard me not; Cleanthes is—
Cleomenes.   He was—no more, good mother;
　　　　　　He tore a piece of me away, and still
　　　　　　The void place aches within me.—O, my boy,
　　　　　　I have bad news to tell thee.
Cleonidas.   None so bad
　　　　　　As that I am a boy.   Cleanthes scorned me;
　　　　　　And, when I drove a thrust, home as I could,
　　　　　　To reach his traitor heart, he put it by,
　　　　　　And cried, as in derision,—Spare the stripling!
　　　　　　Oh that insulting word! I would have swopped
　　　　　　Youth for old age, and all my life behind,
　　　　　　To have been then a momentary man.　(IV. i.)

Nothing could be further from rant, and the play is the least lyrical of all Dryden's tragedies. Many more glorious samples can be fetched from his works, hardly any, perhaps, with fewer deliberate 'poetic beauties': yet it shows, better than other passages could, how important an element the bare word is in Dryden's work, especially when, as here, it is so unobtrusive.

An extract, quoted alone, with nothing especial to recommend it except the very quality it is hoped to show in it, may not be very convincing. A very short passage from Settle, a passage that may compare, in that it attempts no rhetoric or complicated poetic similes, may be to the point:

　　　　　　I, for my former state,
　　　　My homage to your royal father paid,
　　　　For monarchs may destroy what monarchs made:
　　　　For subjects' glories are but borrowed things,
　　　　Raised by the favourable smiles of kings:
　　　　And at their author's pleasure should retire,
　　　　And when their breath renounces 'em, expire.
　　　　　　　　　　(*Empress of Morocco*, III. i.)

In comparing those two, Dryden's achievement is at once visible.

It is easy in Dryden's plays to parallel some of the
piercingly epigrammatic lines with which his satires are
strewn; but the proper wit of a heroic poem, as he remarked in the preface to *Annus Mirabilis,* does not lie in
the jerk or sting of an epigram; in tragedy it is tedious,
and can only exist happily where it is well knit into the
texture of the dialogue. Detached from their setting,
many phrases of Dryden's seem to be epigrams, but in their
place they merely appear as slightly stronger statements,
which is in itself a tribute to the high standard of his dramatic writing. He rarely introduced satire, and where he
did it was moderate and laughter-provoking, rather than
withering. Thus in *Aureng-Zebe* (I):

> The ministers of state, who gave us law,
> In corners with selected friends withdraw:
> There in deaf murmurs, solemnly are wise;
> Whisp'ring like winds, ere hurricanes arise.
> The most corrupt are most obsequious grown,
> And those they scorned officiously they own.

To have been more biting, to have aroused the sort of
excitement produced by *Mac Flecknoe* or *Absalom and
Achitophel* would again have destroyed that balance of
emotions upon which his plays depend.

Dryden is undoubtedly the purest artist of all the
Restoration writers of tragedy, besides being the most
accomplished craftsman. It may be wondered why he, who
stated expressly that plot was not merely a peg to hang fine
things on, should so often have been contented with poor
ones, until we remember that for him plot did not mean
fable: it was definitely the arrangement of emotions that he
meant. Although his work is pretty, it is strong and solid
as well, as it had to be to make the grace bearable. He
was an artist because his eye and his mind were always on

the object made; the general moral of his work might be allowed to take care of itself, to filter in unconsciously through his general temper, which, if anything, was one of tolerant scepticism. For him, as for Hardy, the thing made was to be a presentation of life; but the individual sees life not only through his own temperament but also through the eye of his age. The great statement of tragedy, whether as drama or as novel, 'This is what happens to man', hardly concerned him, and it is really this failure which keeps him out of the company of the very greatest. In truth, he was more eager to note, 'This is what people are like or would wish to be like', which is the observation of a writer of comedy. Nevertheless, just because he did keep his eye on the object, he made things which are alive to-day, and which can still be read for their intrinsic worth, and not merely from the idle curiosity of the student. Of no other writer of tragedy in that age can this be said, except of Otway; but where with Otway it is the realism which tells, with Dryden it is the artificiality which makes permanent.

VI

NAT LEE (1653–1692) AND THE TRAGEDY OF HUMOURS

Nero, 1674.
Sophonisba, 1675.
Gloriana, 1676.
The Rival Queens, 1677.
Mithridates, 1678.
Cæsar Borgia, 1679.
Theodosius, 1680.
Lucius Junius Brutus, 1680.
Constantine the Great, 1683.
The Massacre of Paris, acted 1689.

Then he will talk, good Gods, how he will talk!
(*The Rival Queens,* I.)

IT is impossible to regard Nathaniel (or Nathanael) Lee as a great writer, to join in the opinion sometimes heard that his is the last vaulting flame of Elizabethan inspiration. Violence is not inspiration, nor any crashing noise the voice of Jove. To read him aloud is to stun one's hearers into somnolence, to hypnotize them with an apparently endless flow of high-falutin' words and phrases, trumpeted out so indiscriminately that they gradually become devoid of meaning. Taken in small doses, rant is enlivening, especially when the writer seems so evidently to enjoy it. But what if the rant is invariable and unvaried, if the strain on one's highest fancy (not imagination) is without relaxation? There can be no purple patch where all is incarnadined, and humanity itself is drowned in an ocean of verbiage.

But taken for granted that certain things are expected of his characters; that immaculate ' nobility ', undauntable love, are the order of the day; that the mentality of the figures (if the word 'mentality' can be used of anything so inflexible) is cut and thoroughly dried, out of what can the dramatist create? Words: words detached from any association outside the boundaries of the play. There is nothing else the audience can hope for, no other expectation to keep them alert. The writer, deprived of the resources of psychology, of fear and pity, of surprise and any real conflict, is bound to resort to stunning and hypnotizing. If he can succeed, by the sheer impact of his verbiage, in producing the 'full repose' usually reached by other means, his work is justified. It may be possible for him to create an object by the purely mechanical use of words; and in examining Lee one must judge him by his consistency in this realm, just as, perhaps, we should judge Swinburne. And if he has created an object, we must try to discover what sort of object it is he has created.

Lee is, one may fairly safely say, the most completely 'heroic' of all the outstanding heroic writers, though Banks and Settle, perhaps, run him close. If it is agreed that this type of tragedy explores man's capacity for one form of honour and one form of love, we can say, without fear of serious contradiction, that Lee explored these to the uttermost, and never for a moment stepped off on to any other part of the map. Indeed, with him the word 'explored' hardly seems the right one; it would be better to say 'exploited . Take, for instance, the plot of *Gloriana*:

In Act I we meet Augustus—in a fury. When his adulators try to please him, he tells them to be silent. He is annoyed with Marcellus, partly for his successes in Spain, and partly because he has harboured Cæsario, the son of Julius Cæsar and Cleopatra. He is enraged with his daughter Julia for her 'luxury', and has to be restrained from killing her. When his advisers tell him that he ought to subdue his love for Gloriana,

Pompey's daughter, as being too old for such exercise, he threatens to hew off their heads with his own sword.

Act II opens with Cæsario—in a fury. Augustus has offered a reward for his head. He boasts; he has 'God-like courage'; he performs 'divine acts' in slaying beasts. He horribly draws his sword, and childishly imitates his future slaying of Augustus's guards. Marcellus coming in remarks:

> Ne'er did I see that scabbard empty made,
> But drunken slaughter hung upon the blade.

But Cæsario's 'virtue', namely, his fast bosom friendship for Marcellus, makes him offer to forgo his revenge. 'This is a point too subtle for mankind' is the opinion of Marcellus. The entry of Narcissa brings a little respite, and Cæsario avows himself subdued by 'beauty's batteries'. He has, apparently, never seen her before. After a love-scene prodigal of words, Tiberius comes to tell Marcellus of his wife Julia's extravagances; how in her debauches she flouted even Jove. Then Marcellus lets fly—in a fury, and all the glowing imagery of hell. Julia opportunely appears, and Marcellus has to be restrained from killing her, with her paramour Ovid. Cæsario's sword is drawn on this occasion. Augustus comes in with guards, who disarm all but Cæsario, who will not be disarmed, and, nobly controlling his passion, goes out when Augustus throws a dagger at him.

As the curtain rises on Act III we see Cæsario—in a fury, betraying his vow to Marcellus, and plotting to kill Augustus while at play in his amorous bower. Scene ii, after a delightful Drydenesque song, shows us Augustus in a violent passion of lust, trying to seduce Gloriana, who threatens suicide. Augustus in turn threatens death, but finding that useless, changes his threat to one of rape and forcible feeding. Just after he has gone out Cæsario comes in, and drives his sword through a guardian captain. He and Gloriana fall violently in love with one another at the first glimpse.

Act IV opens with the stage direction, 'Marcellus with his sword drawn against Julia'. However, he relents, overcome by her beauty and her resistlessness. 'Enter Cæsario bloody', with Gloriana and his friends. Marcellus pledges himself to help him against he knows not whom. Narcissa appears, to tell Cæsario that he has been betrayed to Augustus. She observes that Cæsario's affections have been transferred else-where. Augustus comes in, and after some pompous talk orders Cæsario to be taken by his guards. Marcellus steps in to defend him. After mutual recriminations, Augustus feels strong enough to order 'Disarm Marcellus, and Cæsario slay'. Julia and Narcissa fall on their knees and plead. He shortly after tries to rush on Cæsario and kill him himself, but is restrained. He breaks away, but Gloriana, until then veiled, reveals herself and interposes, offering herself in exchange for Cæsario's life. The latter thereupon surrenders his sword. Follows a pretty parting scene between Cæsario and Gloriana.

Act v, Augustus and Narcissa—both in a fury with each other. Narcissa wants Cæsario; Augustus wants to kill him, and match Narcissa suitably. As she goes out Gloriana comes in. Augustus, in a fury of madness, promises her anything—to spare Cæsario, to spill the blood of whole nations; nay, 'speak but the word, the dead, the dead shall die'. Gloriana declares that she loves Augustus, and gets him to promise Cæsario a safe banishment. But Narcissa, who has been listening, interposes as they go out, and raves against both Augustus and Gloriana, the latter having stolen Cæsario's heart from her. After listening for a short time, Augustus aptly remarks:

> Away to some dark room let her be had,
> For either you and I or she is mad.

For some inexplicable and unexplained reason Augustus is struck with dread before the end of the scene, and almost renounces Gloriana, concluding, however, 'Let ruin wait, I'll taste her though I die'. Then, heralded by a charming dulcet song, is a tender, 'noble' scene between Cæsario and Narcissa, but the latter soon rouses Cæsario's fury by telling him that Gloriana is treacherous. He accuses her of lying, whereupon, in spite of Cæsario's remorse, she begins to die of a broken heart. Much moved, the young hero promises to love her, and Narcissa promptly dies of joy. He would like to commit suicide, but no weapon is handy, and his heart, he tells us, is too big to break; 'it must with Fate be rent'. Marcellus then rushes in, telling Cæsario to fly, but seeing his sister dead turns and rends Cæsario, and would kill him but for the young hero being unarmed. Cæsario nobly offers his breast in vain. Julia coming in softens Marcellus's heart, and then Cæsario begs him, as the last office due to their past friendship, to take him where he may 'to Gloriana's guilt appear'. The last scene is in the Emperor's bed-chamber, where we see Gloriana, 'dressed in white, with a dagger in her hand, tapers, &c.' She is going to kill Augustus, thus saving Cæsario and her honour too. She goes to bed. Cæsario enters, so distracted that she thinks it is his ghost. He raves at her for her treachery to him, and as he will not listen to her explanation she stabs herself mortally to convince him. Augustus comes in; a fight ensues, in which Cæsario is killed. Tiberius coming in tells him that Marcellus has died of grief, and that Julia is about to do so. Augustus ends the play by saying that he also will die soon, giving orders for his pyre, naming his successor, and complaining that

> So Heaven abroad with conquest crowns my wars,
> But wracks my spirit with domestic jars.

The last word in the play is the only weak one.

Now, ridiculous as all this may appear, when thus baldly stated, it has not been recounted for the purpose of ridicule. For in actual reading the play is not so absurd as it may sound, and would be less so on the stage. Mighty torrents of rant carry it along. Judged by any standard of reality it would be monstrous enough, but it never comes near enough reality to be judged by such a standard. It is clear, however, that to attempt to relate Lee to Shakespeare is folly; as to say that he is worth more than Ford or Webster, as has recently been said (astonishing as it may seem), is unthinkable. But there is something there. One does feel, after reading one of his plays, that some sort of object has been created. It is not a pretty object, like one of Dryden's; it is a grotesque of heroic tragedy worth looking at, however, because it obeys laws of its own. Granted the scheme on which it is made, it is well proportioned; the detail is good, and all of a piece. The lights are very high (they are reflected from metal), and the shadows are very dark. It is Gothic building run mad, but it retains the virtues of

Gothic, being held up by terrific stresses, and towering up above the mundane street.

According to Addison : 'Among our English poets, there was none who was better turned for tragedy than Lee, if instead of favouring the impetuosity of his genius, he had restrained it, and kept it within proper bounds. His thoughts are wonderfully suited to tragedy, but frequently lost in such a cloud of words that it is hard to see the beauty of them: there is an infinite fire in his works, but so involved in smoke that it does not appear in half its lustre.' Addison had a better chance of judging than we have, since he must often have seen Lee upon the stage ; but we may venture to doubt whether, had the clouds of words been absent, the thoughts would have seemed so wonderfully suited to tragedy. For the clouds themselves are the thoughts. Certainly Lee did not much dally with poetic justice. He could write verse ; he was prolific of imagery ; and he could recognize the things which ought to be tragic. But take away the plethora of words, leave him only such psychological handling as he was capable of, such subtlety of emotion as he could portray, and his tragedies would be lamentable indeed. Feeling the force of words, he built out of them: it is no mere accident that he twice collaborated with Dryden, in *Œdipus* and in *The Duke of Guise.*

But if both relied upon words as their chief instrument, where of course they differ is in what they tried to make words do: they were not really fitting duettists. Dryden's voice, though virile, is sweet ; Lee's is a terrific ' hollow ', to use a favourite word of his. Thus the atmospheres of *Œdipus* are strikingly incongruous. Acts I and III have all Dryden's mellowness, the remainder the harsh, grinding tones of Lee—the tones of a man who, if not mad (his confinement in Bedlam may have been due to *delirium tremens*), would try to exacerbate his audience to madness. Let us compare the two in the play, merely for the words, and not for the grace which distinguishes Dryden, or the welter of blood, the concentration of Grand Guignol horror which marks the ending by Lee:

> The Gods are just.———
> But how can finite measure infinite?
> Reason! alas, it does not know itself!
> Yet man, vain man, would with this short-lined plummet
> Fathom the vast abyss of heavenly justice.
> Whatever is, is in its causes just;
> Since all things are by Fate. But purblind man
> Sees but a part o' th' chain, the nearest links;
> His eyes not carrying to that equal beam
> That poises all above.   (Act III.)

> Sure, 'tis the end of all things! Fate has torn
> The lock of Time off, and his head is now
> The ghastly ball of round eternity!
> Call you these peals of thunder but the yawn
> Of bellowing clouds? By Jove, they seem to me
> The world's last groans; and those vast sheets of flame
> Are all its blaze! The tapers of the Gods,
> The sun and moon, run down like waxen globes;
> The shooting stars end all in purple jellies,
> And chaos is at hand.   (Opening of Act II.)

Lee is always at the extremity of passion; there is no measure in him: his fancy is ever at full gallop, and there is no judgement to lay hold upon the reins. His people are all madmen in fact, even if they are not, like Britannicus in *Nero* and Nero himself, 'distracted'. They hurtle and bang across the stage, and when they meet are immediately fast locked in love or friendship, or rush upon each other with swords and daggers. But we expect it of them. Their words and actions have all the infernal consistency of madness, a logic which ignores the checks of actual life. The frequent imprecation, slightly varied, 'Night, horror,

death, confusion, hell and furies', is a kind of *leit-motiv*
running through all Lee's work, even in his semi-comic
The Princess of Cleves. The atmosphere he produces is that
of a stage hothouse; the tension is so great that if anything
were at any moment to relax, the whole structure would
collapse to the ground. That it does not collapse is evidence of some queer driving power in the man—a power in
many ways admirable.

It is likely that he himself sometimes felt that the pace
was too hot to last, for he often introduces portentous
shows, or pieces of ritual, which, while they do not relax
the tension, at least vary it, and slow down the tumultuous
action. In the same way he occasionally slackens the pace
of his rhymed verse by introducing the quatrain. His songs
are often charming, and in their changes of rhythm are
reminiscent of Dryden. As good a one as any from this
point of view is the duet between the ghosts of Darius
and Queen Statira in *The Rival Queens, or Alexander the
Great*:

Dar.	Is innocence so void of cares,
	That it can undisturbed sleep
	Amidst the noise of horrid wars,
	That make immortal spirits weep?
Stat.	No boding crows, nor raven come,
	To warn her of approaching doom.
Dar.	She walks, as she dreams, in a garden of flowers,
	And her hands are employed in the beautiful bowers;
	She dreams of the man that is far from the grove,
	And all her lost fancy still runs on her love.
Stat.	She nods o'er the brooks that run purling along,
	And the nightingales lull her more fast with a song.
Dar.	But see the sad end which the Gods have decreed.
Stat.	This poinard's thy fate.
Dar.	My daughter must bleed.
Chorus.	Awake then, Statira, awake, for alas you must die;
	E'er an hour be past, you must breathe out your last.

Dar. And be such another as I.
Stat. As I.
Dar. And be such another as I.

The effect is curiously operatic, and one may well wonder whether Lee might not, in fact, have been an operatic genius who mistook his medium. His plays in their whole tenor, their form, their extravagance, would seem to lend themselves amazingly well to music of a pseudo-Wagnerian sort. It may be that with music the songs in the plays may have seemed more congruous with the dialogue; but in the reading their gay lyrical lilt, though it comes as pleasurable relief, seems at variance with the thunderous gloom, lightning-streaked though it be, of most of his scenes. Gloom, indeed, is too weak a word; the blackness of hell would be more fitting, and nearer, probably, to what he aimed at. Thus the songs have no literary connexion with the plays.

There is no need to stress the word 'mad', but there is no denying the fact that Lee was shut away for five years, and that the epithet was applied to him by his contemporaries. His work, as Steele remarked, illustrates 'passion in its purity, without mixture of reason'. His unbalanced megalomaniacs 'boil like drunkards' veins' with 'Gothic fury'; and we may quote a passage not so violent as the one referred to by Steele (*Spectator*, 438) to point the comment:

Alexander. Yes, I will shake this Cupid from my arms.
If all the rages of the earth would fright him;
Drown him in the deep bowl of Hercules;
Make the world drunk, and then like Æolus,
When he gave passage to the struggling winds,
I'll strike my spear into the reeling globe
To let it blood, set Babylon in a blaze,
And drive this God of flames with more consuming
fires.   (*The Rival Queens*, III. i.)

This, after all, is not much saner than the ravings of Caesar Borgia when in the delirium of death from poison :

Ange. Where are our guards?
Borgia. Hark, I hear 'em coming;
      Or is it dooms-day? ha—— by hell, it is;
      And see, the heavens, and earth, and air, are all
      On fire; the very seas, like molten glass,
      Roll their bright waves, and from the smoky deep
      Cast up the glaring dead. . .   (*Cæsar Borgia*, v. ii.)

and so on. We get something of portents and prodigies in Shakespeare, as in *Julius Caesar*; but whereas in Shakespeare they are put in for the sake of the atmosphere, to produce a sense of uneasiness, of the womb of time being ripe with some terrible birth, with Lee they are crammed in for their own sake. But with the latter the fury of vision, the extravagance of action is absorbed in the violence of the words. In the same play Bellamira, when she wishes to say that she is obedient to her father, remarks that she has

           torn off my breasts,
      My breasts, my very heart, and flung it from me,
      To feed the tyrant Duty with my blood.

There are moments, naturally, if not of relaxation at least of a more normal sombreness, an attempt to get away from the torture of the instant to something more general, as in the Duke of Gandia's farewell to and renunciation of Bellamira, or in the phrases of Machiavelli, surely the most machiavellian Machiavelli ever drawn :

      The dead are only happy, and the dying :
      The dead are still, and lasting slumbers hold 'em :
      He who is near his death but turns about,
      Shuffles awhile to make his pillow easy,
      Then slips into his shroud, and rests for ever.   (III. i.)

But such passages are, as it were, only momentary lapses:

> Look, a poor lunatic that makes his moan,
> And for a time beguiles the lookers on,
> He reasons well, his eyes their wildness lose,
> And vows his keepers his wronged sense abuse :
> But if you hit the cause that hurts his brain,
> Then his teeth gnash, he foams, he shakes his chain,
> His eyeballs roll, and he is mad again.   (v. i.)

It is as though when certain subjects came up for treatment in the course of one of Lee's plays he could not control himself. Then, only the extreme, only the absolute, could satisfy him. And since the 'Roman' ideal is not among the usual passions, one may take his reaction to it as an example of his extreme trend. For him nothing was Roman but what was so harsh and unfeeling as to be inhuman. In *Lucius Junius Brutus*, what appealed to him in Brutus was not his sense of justice, nor his patriotism, but his severity to his sons—a severity deliberately made shocking in the play, by showing that the judicial murder of one of his sons was quite unnecessary, Romanism for Romanism's sake, and not for Rome's. This Lee calls 'old Roman gold'. In *Constantine the Great* Dalmatius will ruthlessly execute Lycinius in view of his friends, to show the youthful Annibal 'a pattern of the old Romans'. These are by no means the only instances. Certainly, if that was the Restoration ideal of Rome, one can only be glad that it was not realized. The Tarpeian rock would have been an uncomfortable substitute for Whitehall.

Yet, it must be insisted, all this fury and violence, this extravagant action, this talk washed in 'tuns of blood' to the accompaniment of gnashing teeth, has a certain coherence, a validity of its own. It is all of a piece. A heroic play by Lee is not unlike a heroic picture by Haydon, a man whose megalomania much resembles Lee's. He also was for 'High Art' as against mere representation of life. Yet neither thought he was misrepresenting Nature: he was refining it. So Haydon, who rejected Fuseli's 'Damn Nature! she always puts me out' position, wrote: 'We have no business to make Nature as she never was: all we have to do is to restore her to what she is according to the definite principles of *her first creation.*' And Lee, in the Dedication of *Lucius Junius Brutus*: 'The poet must elevate his fancy with the mightiest imagination; he must run back so many hundred years, take a just prospect of those times, without the least thought of ours; for, if his eye should swerve so low, his muse will grow giddy with the vastness of the distance, fall at once, and for ever lose the majesty of *the first design.*' Haydon felt that the figure of his Dentatus must be heroic, and the finest specimen of the species he could invent. But how, he asked, was he to build a heroic form, above life, yet like life? That must have been precisely Lee's attitude with, say, Mithridates. He would have agreed with Fuseli that a subject should always astonish or surprise. He would have sympathized with Haydon in trying to 'attain that breadth of form and style so essential to the heroic', and approved of his addition of 'some light airy ostrich feathers which give a more ponderous look to my hero'. There must be no discordant note in Haydon's picture: the murderers in *Dentatus* must be given 'as much personal beauty as is not quite inconsistent with their work. If they had all possessed the expression of murderers it might have been more true, but who could have dwelt upon it with pleasure?' Lee did not mind making his murderers murderer-like, but there must be no break in the surface. So, in the Dedication already quoted, 'There must be no dross throughout the whole mass, the furnace must be justly heated, and the bullion stamped with an unerring hand '. So far good ; this will account for his work. But then : ' In such writing there must be greatness of thought without bombast, remoteness without monstrousness ; virtue armed with severity, not in iron bodice . . . speaking out without cracking the voice or straining the lungs.' It is a pity he did not apply his own precepts ; he admits to being a lag in the race, but the truth is, he ran too far ahead.

Yet he brought every one of his imaginary figures with him ; they all spoke in the same cracked voice, so the atmosphere is maintained, even though it be a riven atmosphere. If by saying that Lee had good ' thoughts ' for tragedy Addison meant that he had an eye for a situation, and a knowledge of what ought to go to compose one, he was right. Although the verbiage seems to be the thought, it is just possible that had the words been toned down the emotions might have seemed congruous with the facts. There is stuff in Lee, and he took great stories to build on, though he did not hesitate to alter the foundations if it suited him to do so. The situations in which his people struggle are often those about which a fuss can legitimately be made ; they are not dependent merely upon fantastic ideas of honour, though these are not absent. His mistake was, rather, to make his people act and speak all the while ' in character ', so that they seem possessed by one absorbing idea, with the result that we seem to be moving in a world of tragic ' humours ', where the ' excess ', instead of being exposed to cure by laughter, is held up to admiration, or used to promote revulsion. His appeal to pity is more legitimate than that of most of his contemporaries ; it is not only the pity which was considered due to misfortune in love, though, on the other hand, it is apt to be slightly sentimentalized. The persons, mainly women, whom he used for pity have a certain charm, but they do not interest us enough to make us feel the real tragic pity, which consists in realizing that something fine is marred or destroyed.

His attempts to relieve his sulphurous atmosphere with ' poetic beauties' are not unpleasing, but they do not last long, and are seldom uttered in his own cracked voice. It was not he but Shakespeare who wrote, or nearly wrote:

> Alcides, I and thou, my dearest Theseus,
> When through the woods we chased the foaming boar,
> With hounds that opened like Thessalian bulls,
> Like tigers flued, and sanded as the shore,
> With ears and chests that dashed the morning dew.
>
> > (*Theodosius*, I. i.)

while there are cribs from *The Tempest*, echoes from *Hamlet* and *Lear*. When we listen to the dying Teraminta saying:

> Oh, I grope about
> But cannot find thee,

we know we are listening to Beaumont and Fletcher's Aspatia moaning:

> Give me thy hand, my hands grope up and down
> And cannot find thee,

and so on. Certainly Lee, in prefacing *Mithridates*, said that he had based himself on Shakespeare and Fletcher—on the first for Roman greatness, and on the second for sweetness; and there is no harm in theft if you can better the thing stolen. But with Lee it never is bettered. Thus there are vague reminiscences of Webster in *Constantine the Great* which are merely floating references; and when the dying Alexander in *The Rival Queens* shouts ' Victoria, Victoria, Victoria', there seems to be no earthly reason for his doing so but that Brachiano in *The White Devil* shouts

' Vittoria ! Vittoria ! ' when he is done to death. Yet he was well advised to get his good things where he could find them, for his own ' poetic beauties ' are not always happy.

> His pretty eyes, ruddy and wet with tears
> Like two burst cherries rolling in a storm

is not the luckiest of images. He was better at the descriptive adjective, such as ' headlong Alexander ', or the arrowy line, as, for example :

> And guilt, like wildfire, thrilled him as he spoke,

which is strong enough for most listeners, but lamentably weak when judged by his own standards.

His most popular play, and in many ways his best, is *The Rival Queens*, which has at least left the often mis-quoted line, ' When Greeks joined Greeks, then was the tug of war ', to dwell in the common memory. It is the story of the rivalry of the two queens of Alexander the Great, and though the plot is tumultuous and contorted enough (Lee's knots are cut rather than unravelled, and by very irresponsible shears), there is much dignity, while the words rise less often to melodramatic exuberance. Some lines of the most famous scene, that of the second meeting of the rival queens, deserve quotation here, so as to show Lee at his best. Statira, having fallen out of Alexander's love, because he has been re-enthralled by his first wife, Roxana, is about to depart to a cloistered life, in spite of the arguments of the royal mother, Sysigambis, when she meets Roxana. The latter at first is all pity, but then cannot forbear gibing at her fallen foe, who then changes her mind, and determines after all to try to win Alexander back. The psychology of the scene has been attacked, yet it is plain and plausible enough. But to claim that it is profoundly subtle, of a subtlety 'rarely discovered in dramatists other than Shakespeare', is to lose one's sense of humour. But perhaps, really to appreciate Lee, one should aim at a temporary suspension of the sense of humour. At all events here is the last, and best, part of the scene: the first part is more moderately worded, and therefore, since it is Lee, seems a little dead:

Roxana.   Madam, I hope you will a queen forgive :
        Roxana weeps to see Statira grieve :
        How noble is the brave resolve you make,
        To quit the world for Alexander's sake !
        Vast is your mind, you dare thus greatly die,
        And yield the king to one so mean as I :
        'Tis a revenge will make the victor smart,
        And much I fear your death will break his heart.

Statira.   You counterfeit, I fear, and know too well
        How much your eyes all beauties else excel :
        Roxana, who tho' not a princess born,
        In chains could make the mighty victor mourn.
        Forgetting pow'r when wine had made him warm,
        And senseless, yet even then you knew to charm :
        Preserve him by those arts that cannot fail,
        While I the loss of what I loved bewail.

Roxana.   I hope your majesty will give me leave
        To wait you to the grove, where you would grieve ;
        Where, like the turtle, you the loss will moan
        Of that dear mate, and murmur all alone.

Statira.   No, proud triumpher o'er my fallen state,
        Thou shalt not stay to fill me with my fate :
        Go to the conquest which your wiles may boast,
        And tell the world you left Statira lost.
        Go seize my faithless Alexander's hand,
        Both hand and heart were once at my command :
        Grasp his loved neck, die on his fragrant breast,⎫
        Love him like me whose love can't be exprest, ⎬
        He must be happy, and you more than blest ;
        While I in darkness hide me from the day,⎫
        That with my mind I may his form survey,⎬
        And think so long, till I think life away. ⎭

Roxana. No, sickly virtue, no,
  Thou shalt not think, nor thy love's loss bemoan,
  Nor shall past pleasures through thy fancy run;
  That were to make thee blest as I can be:
  But thy no-thought I must, I will decree;
  And thus, I'll torture thee till thou art mad,
  And then no thought to purpose can be had.

Statira. How frail, how cowardly is woman's mind!
  We shriek at thunder, dread the rustling wind,
  And glitt'ring swords the brightest eyes will blind.
  Yet glitt when strong jealousy enflames the soul,
  The weak will roar, and calms to tempests roll.
  Rival, take heed, and tempt me not too far;
  My blood may boil, and blushes show a war.

Roxana. When you retire to your romantic cell
  I'll make thy solitary mansion hell;
  Thou shalt not rest by day, nor sleep by night,
  But still Roxana shall thy spirit fright:
  Wanton in dreams if thou dar'st dream of bliss,
  Thy roving ghost may think to steal a kiss;
  But when to his sought bed, thy wand'ring air
  Shall for the happiness it wished repair,
  How will it groan to find thy rival there!
  How ghastly wilt thou look, when thou shalt see,
  Through the drawn curtains, that great man and me,
  Wearied with laughing, joys shot to the soul,
  While thou shalt grinning stand, and gnash thy teeth,
    and howl?

Statira. O barb'rous rage! my tears I cannot keep,
  But my full eyes in spite of me will weep.

Roxana. The king and I in various pictures drawn,
  Clasping each other, shaded o'er with lawn,
  Shall be the daily presents I will send,
  To help thy sorrow to her journey's end.
  And when we hear at last thy hour draws nigh,
  My Alexander, my dear love and I,
  Will come and hasten on thy ling'ring fates,
  And smile and kiss thy soul out through the grates.

Statira. 'Tis well, I thank thee; thou hast waked a rage,
  Whose boiling now no temper can assuage:
  I meet thy tides of jealousy with more,
  Dare thee to duel, and dash thee o'er and o'er.

Roxana. What would you dare?
Statira. Whatever you dare do,
 My warring thoughts the bloodiest tracts pursue;
 I am by love a Fury made, like you:
 Kill or be killed, thus acted by despair.
Roxana. Sure the disdained Statira does not dare?
Statira. Yes, tow'ring proud Roxana, but I dare.
Roxana. I tow'r indeed o'er thee;
 Like a fair wood, the shade of kings I stand,
 While thou, sick weed, dost but infest the land.
Statira. No, like an ivy I will curl thee round,
 Thy sapless trunk of all its pride confound,
 Then dry and withered, bend thee to the ground.
 What Sysigambis' threats, objected fears,
 My sister's sighs, and Alexander's tears
 Could not effect, thy rival rage has done;
 My soul, whose start at breach of oaths begun,
 Shall to thy ruin violated run.
 I'll see the king, in spite of all I swore,
 Though curst, that thou may'st never see him more.

(III. i.)

It has a certain amount of life, and even feeling, though
rather crude, for Lee's values are always sensual values;
but it will not stand a moment's comparison with the
scene between Cleopatra and Octavia in *All for Love*. The
fact is that Lee is most himself when he is dealing in
superlatives, when no word can be too strong, no image
too tremendous:

 Far from the guilt of palaces, oh send me!
 Drive me, oh drive me from the traitor man.
 So I might 'scape that monster, let me dwell
 In lions' haunts or in some tiger's den;
 Place me on some steep, craggy, ruined rock,
 That bellies out, just dropping on the ocean;
 Bury me in the hollow of its womb,
 Where starving on my cold and flinty bed
 I may from far, with giddy apprehension,
 See infinite fathoms down the rumbling deep;
 Yet not ev'n there, in that vast whirl of death,

> Can there be found so terrible a ruin
> As man, false man, smiling destructive man.

To enjoy Lee, and he can be enjoyed, the reader must abandon himself on the rushing river of words, half-images, and shadowy generalizations.

When all is said, the final test of a drama is its own peculiar quality of life, its capacity for existing side by side with what we know as reality. It cannot be utterly different from reality, since a work of art is unavoidably composed of the same elements as life. There is a distinction between art and life, but in the works of a master it is never easy to see why the symbol is not life, or how it is that the life shown swells into a symbol. Lee's plays are not like life ; but no doubt he meant them to be symbolic of it. Where he failed was to make the distinction between art and life while at the same time concealing the point of divergence. The attempt is not isolated, and is likely to be made at periods of disordered values, and it is of this, rather than of his own madness, that Lee's plays are symptomatic. At the present day his writings may be paralleled by the hysterical ravings of Herr Fritz von Unruh. What saved Lee was the form imposed upon him by his time, and its values, however factitious they may have been. Had he lived to-day he would, one may guess, have joined the ranks of the Expressionists, and striven to create a new form in a world of drama where we ‘ sit and wait, old broken tables around us, and also half-written tables’. With some artists, however, it may be only gain to be bound by strict limitations of form, though all matter must be open to them, and this was probably the case with Lee.

One can say of Expressionism that it is at least a plucky attempt to orientate the drama in a world where no values

are universally accepted. It is an attempt at creation out
of the void; but the result is that the authors seem to be
trying to express something which lies beyond experience.
This is precisely what we feel with Lee. In the Expressionists' attempt to do without values, they are trying to
state absolute truth, just as Lee was trying to do with
artificial values. But seeing that truth is a dubious thing,
what is interesting is the emotions which gather round a
'truth'; and again, given that the mere statement of
'truth' is of no artistic value, it is the movement of the
mind between 'truths' that is important. In the Expres-
sionist plays we do not feel that we have passed through
any experience, or submitted to that organization of the
impulses which leads to a 'full repose'. That is not quite
the state of affairs with Lee, because with him the form
itself produces certain definite results.

Although the likeness between Lee and the Expressionists must not be pushed too far, it is worth while to consider the latter a little further, if only to indicate points of
divergence, or to suggest where the new way of writing
might have been useful to the former. The justification of
the modern way of writing, if it needs one, as well as of
its name, is, possibly, to be found in Signor Croce's *Aesthetic*, in which 'art' means 'vision' or 'intuition'. It
has not the character of conceptual knowledge; and, on
this scheme, intuition means no less than the indistinction
of reality and unreality, which would certainly cover Lee's
vision. 'Ideality', Signor Croce says, 'is the intimate
virtue of art, and no sooner are reflection and judgement
developed from that ideality, than art is dissipated and dies.'
So far this will cover both Lee and the Expressionists (it
would have horrified Dryden and Rymer); but, Signor
Croce goes on to say that unity is essential, for, 'a series

of images which seem to be, each in turn, convincingly powerful, leaves us nevertheless deluded and diffident '. Precisely ; and this is what occurs with the Expressionists. With Lee, however, there is unity, even if it is a somewhat artificial one ; felt, that is, to be artificial, and not conveying that sense of organic growth which we recognize in the works of the masters. But if, with the Expressionists, you are intellectually a nihilist, where is unity to come from ? There appears to be no direction at all in the thought of Herr Toller, or Herr Kaiser. It is this, rather than the disjuncted form of the plays, that is ruinous. It may, perhaps, be possible to create without a background of values, but in that case direction must be given by the presence of emotion profound and ordered.

In Lee, it may be, the emotion is profound enough, but it is only ordered by the artificial form—and the artificial formulas. This is a weakness, since, for the creator, not *de la forme naît l'idée* is true, but the reverse. Yet it saved him. And moreover, where he gains over the Expressionists is in his use of rhetoric. The ' form ' they have evolved gives enormous scope for this, but it is the very advantage which they do not seize. Herr Toller shows signs in that direction, but he is very mouthy, as is probably inevitable if you do not believe in the importance of anything you say. Lee is not merely mouthy; he justifies his rhetoric by trying to express the absolute. Everything goes to show that the form and ideas of his age were the very things by which he lived. Yet both his plays and those of the Expressionists are plays of life approached from a bewildered intellectual angle. Lee's are an attempt at adjustment in a world of heroic thoughts, Herr Toller's of adjustment in a world of mass emotions, but both try to deal direct with the symbol, and expect life to emerge from it, which is fatal. It is not enough for an audience to be plunged into a world of extreme heroic feelings, outrageous love at first sight, patriotism which overwhelms all human feeling, bravery which ignores the object for which it sacrifices itself, any more than it is enough to be bombarded with antitheses, such as Free-Unfree, Masses-Man, or to be told by Herr Kaiser of the Guilt of All Life, of Eternal Recurrence (chiefly of Stupidity), or be shown a vision of Man Perpetually Crucified. In neither case will abstractions do: it is always the simple word, the familiar material action which counts. ' Ye who govern the mighty world and its mighty concerns with the engines of eloquence— who heat it and cool it, and melt it—and then harden it again to your purpose . . . .—meditate—meditate, I beseech you, upon Trim's hat!'

THOMAS OTWAY (1652-85)

Poetarum qui in Britannia enotuerunt, facile principis, his tombstone declares, and with reference to his age, the claim can be supported; in fact, as far as the drama goes, remains almost undisputed. He is of the first, if not the first, for if he had something which Dryden had not, he lacked something which Dryden possessed (though Pope would not credit the latter with it), namely, the art to blot. His excess was not one of words only, but of ideas which he made use of to pad out or clothe other ideas not in themselves strong or beautiful enough to stand naked. His extravagance is unlike Lee's; it is not one of madness (a neurosis of strength, Nietzsche might have called it), but rather of softness. That is, he could have afforded to blot, as Lee could not have; his work would have come out stronger, not feebler. He exhibits fairly clearly, but less consciously than most, the accepted heroic values of his time, the strained 'Romanism', the idea of valour, and especially the piteousness of unhappy love: but he stands out from his contemporaries—he is probably the most read of them nowadays—because he is less artificial than they are. This is both a virtue, for the obvious reason that his plays are a more direct reaction to life; and a weakness, because he could not free himself enough from his own emotions to make his tragedies objects in themselves.

For, if Otway was much the child of his age in regard to his general attitude towards life, he was never altogether easy in the garb the criticism, both theoretic and popular, of his day expected him to wear. Obedient to a classical training, eager no doubt to follow the great figures of his age and to please his patrons, he at first tried to bend his too profuse emotions into the fashionable formulas. His experiments in heroic couplets are rarely happy, for a successful tragedy in this manner requires a sustained artifice of which he was incapable: allow the natural, simple, forceful phrasing for which he was afterwards to be praised by Addison, to creep in, and the structure vanishes. In his first play, indeed, he was guilty of absurdities almost as gross as those of Sedley in his *Antony and Cleopatra*, and we cannot forbear smiling at:

Theramnes. Heavens, can she at those chains she gave me scoff!
Timandra. You, at your pleasure, Sir, may shake 'em off.

Yet even in this first play, written in the difficult medium at the age of twenty-three, there are some excellent passages wherever love or admiration is involved.

It may be as well to run rapidly over the state of criticism at this time, to see whereabouts Otway was, and what his problem was likely to be. Criticism in the main, as is not to be wondered at, had become something too harsh and narrow, for the Jacobean vine, having run most dismally and weakly riotous, had needed severe pruning. Unfortunately, in their desire to reach coherence, to improve the language of the medium, the writers in the ' new way' took the reactions of the soul for granted; and as one consequence, they had, in their efforts to find a satisfactory form, separated tragedy and comedy into compartments a little too rigid for the English mind. They interpreted Aristotle too literally; tragedy was concerned only with great persons, those, that is, who had exalted titles: comedy dealt with what was low and ridiculous, and everybody could recognize the low. Their idea of tragi-comedy was a play in which the two elements should violently alternate, and they were far from conceiving a fused whole such as Chapman's *The Widow's Tears*, or Shakespeare's *Troilus and Cressida*, of which Dryden gave a completely tragic version. Thus, for them, everything which strayed outside the obvious, one might say the regulation, emotions, they regarded as extravagant, not in accordance with sense, or in bad taste. Any wandering outside the strict forms was a weakness. This, of course, is not to state the whole truth, but it was in the main the current of thought in which Otway found himself when he emerged from his university career in 1671, without taking a degree, to assault the wits and the theatres.

From the first he seems to have been in rebellion against the coffee-house pundits, and the 'youths that newly're come from France', who would sedulously echo the sayings of their betters. Yet the French drama was his earliest allegiance, and if he was not above slightly 'improving' Racine in his *Titus*, there can be no doubt that he owed an enormous debt to ' the author of the French Berenice '. But where he is most conspicuously French he is most evidently immature, and in his first three tragedies we feel that he is putting himself to school, giving us appreciations of poetic sensibility rather than creative work. This was to come later, when, miserably tossed upon a sea of intense and unruly passions, he had acquired a definite and personal attitude towards life, which could not be expressed in any borrowed form, and which he did not live long enough to control into a completely ordered one. Only in versification did the French influence remain, if we are to regard as French the discipline of heroic rhyme ; for although, .

following the lead given by Lee and Dryden, he wrote his
last three tragedies in blank verse, it was a verse which still
retained something of the rigour of the couplet. Thus the
later Otway is unmistakably English : to all seeming he has
lost every foreign taint, and Pope was to write :

> Not but the tragic spirit was our own,
> And full in Shakespeare, fair in Otway shone :

while it has long been customary commonplace that he
returned to the Elizabethans. Yet the change is not immediately a question of form, for to the end he retained
the tighter structure ; it begins to show itself in the kind
of emotion presented, for which he might in the end have
had to find a freer vehicle than that which his age demanded.

His adaptation of Racine's *Bérénice* is interesting, not
so much as a standard of comparison between the two
authors, as in providing a test of the difference between the
two audiences. Otway contracts the play from five acts to
three, not so much by cutting out events, which he does
on occasion, but by reducing the length of the speeches.
There are none of those marvellous, dramatically passionate
tirades which are the essence of Racine, as much as is his
brilliant terseness on occasion : and it is lucky that there
should be none of these, since for anybody else to try to do
what Racine did is either dreariness or disaster. Some of
the time gained, however, he gave back by pulling out
exclamations into speeches, so that the magnificent tension
is lost, and nothing is given in exchange. Where he
‘ improved ’ he naturally ruined, sacrificing Racine's truth
to nature, his reality of emotion, to heroic claptrap. So,

> Il ne m'a retenu que pour parler de vous

becomes

> Tyrranic fair, 'tis true,
> He kept me here only to talk of you :

and the next remark

> De moi, prince ?

is transformed into

> Of me, my lord! forbear this courtly art,
> You're brave and should not mock an easy heart;
> In my distress what pleasure could you see ?
> Alas! or what could Titus say of me ?

To give the sort of effect of general weakening which goes on throughout the adaptation, the cooling down of Racine's livid flame of passion into the smokiness of this ' last of the Elizabethans ', one may quote a short passage from the opening of Racine's Act IV, which is the opening of Act III with Otway. The first speech in either case is omitted :

Bérénice.	Chère Phénice, hé bien! as-tu vu l'empereur ? Qu'a-t-il dit ? Viendra-t-il ?
Phénice.	Oui, je l'ai vu madame, Et j'ai peint à ses yeux le trouble de votre âme J'ai vu couler des pleurs qu'il voudrait retenir.
Bérénice.	Vient-il ?
Phénice.	N'en doutez point, madame, il va venir. Mais voulez-vous paraître en ce désordre extrême ? Remettez-vous, madame, et rentrez en vous-même. Laissez-moi relever ces voiles détachés, Et ces cheveux épars dont vos yeux sont cachés. Souffrez que de vos pleurs je répare l'outrage.
Bérénice.	Laisse, laisse, Phénice, il verra son ouvrage, Et que m'importe, hélas, de ces vains ornements ? Si ma foi, si mes pleurs, si mes gémissements, Mais que dis-je, mes pleurs ? si ma perte certaine, Si ma mort toute prête enfin ne le ramène, Dis-moi, que produiront tes secours superflus, Et tout ce faible éclat qui ne le touche plus ?

Berenice.	Phœnicia, well, my Titus hast thou seen ? What ? will he come and make me live again ?
Phœnicia.	Madam, the Emperor I alone did find; And saw in his the trouble of your mind ; I saw the tears he would have hid, run down.

Berenice.	But was he not ashamed they should be shown ?
	Looked he not as he thought his love disgrace ?
	And was not all the Emperor in his face ?
Phœnicia.	Doubt it not, Madam, he will soon be here :
	But wherefore will you this disorder wear ?
	Your rifled dress let me in order place,
	And these dishevelled locks that hide your face.
Berenice.	Forbear, Phœnicia, let it all alone :
	No, he shall see the triumph he has won ;
	How vain these foolish ornaments must prove,
	If neither faith, nor tears, nor means can move.

He shortens just where he should let himself expand, and
lengthens just where he should be pithy. It is not, of
course, fair to judge Otway from an early play, where his
pen was still pupil ; but it serves to illustrate two things,
namely the deliberate falsification of emotion in the period,
and the futility of an Englishman trying to write like a
Frenchman. Otway had other qualities, which when he
had freed himself from his apprenticeship, he developed
into something very much worth while. Nations gain
nothing by imitating each other's style ; they gain only
from absorbing each other's thought in so far as it may be
universal : for style is not thought and personality only, it
is these plus the literary tradition of the country to which
the writer belongs.

Before going on to examine Otway's tragedies—and it
is by his tragedies that he retained a constant popularity
throughout the eighteenth century, and because of them
that Lamb loved him—it is worth while to glance at his
comedies. His first, an adaptation of *Les Fourberies de
Scapin*, suffers from an attempt to make it more plausible
than the original. Otway, in fact, tried to turn farce,
dealing, in Dryden's phrase, with what was 'monstrous
and chimerical', into a comedy, and the result is not
altogether happy. *Friendship in Fashion* (1678) has little to

recommend it; it has all the ill-nature of Restoration comedy without any of the fairy wit of Etherege, or the mournful grace of Congreve, and he grinds his way mercilessly through. But his next comedy, *The Soldier's Fortune* (1681), is an extraordinary document, which must be understood if an insight is to be obtained into the emotional material which forms the basis of his later tragedy. It centres not only about the bitterness of the discarded soldier, but also about the agony of the flouted lover, and is French only in its adaptation of certain scenes from *L'École des Maris*, and from *Les Amours des Dames Illustres de Notre Siècle*, though it contains borrowings from Fletcher also, and perhaps from Etherege. But in fundamental matter it is nearer Wycherley, recording the struggles of a man whose hopes and faiths are seared with white-hot iron, and who therefore can see mankind only as something despicable and vile. It is a terrible comedy of disillusion. In it Otway reacted much in the same way as Wycherley did to the society of his time, but he had not the native strength to adapt himself, so that his comedy throughout is a poignant *cri de cœur*, sharpened with touches of autobiography: unlike his master in this kind, he could not intellectualize his hurt, nor project it into art. And in this play also we hear the Elizabethan note, for the play has not the movement of its period so much as that of Middleton or Marston, while its raging irony reminds us of the ghastly comic scenes of a tragedy of Ford. Its sequel, *The Atheist*, once more from Scarron, is only more unlucky in its disordered attempt at fantasy, for Otway could not weld together grimness, romance, and laughter. Nothing, indeed, can show more plainly than the development of his comedies, how incongruous a figure he was in the Restoration period—for instance, a much lesser man,

Southerne, succeeded where he failed—and how little
the dramatic mould of his time could suit his quivering
sensibility.

For the story of his life shows him to have been, not so
much an Elizabethan, as a forerunner of the passionate and
romantic lovers of the eighteenth century, with just that
introverted *sensiblerie* more easily discovered in French
memoirs than in English biographies. He was, in fact, a
sentimentalist in a way the Elizabethans were not, or do
not appear to have been from their major works. Shortly
after coming to London he met Mrs. Barry, who usually
acted in his plays, and he fell hopelessly and irremeably
in love with this fascinating but callous creature, who,
however consummate an artist she may have been, preferred
the more robust—one might almost say robustious—
affections of Etherege and Rochester to the more delicate
and certainly less advantageous homage of the best poet
of the three. Unable or unwilling to forbid approaches,
she kept the unfortunate Otway in a state of suspense
which drove him to distraction. This was the central
experience which determined his outlook and his mentality;
it made him the poet he was, though in destroying the man
it may have stifled a still greater poet. At last, unable
any longer to bear a fruitless courtship, in 1678 he accepted
a cornet's commission, and went to Flanders, where

> With the discharge of passions much opprest,
> Disturbed in brain and pensive in his breast,
> Full of those thoughts which make th'unhappy sad,
> And by imagination half grown mad,
> The poet led abroad his mourning muse.

To any one who reads his six letters to Mrs. Barry this does
not seem an overstatement, while the fact that it should be
placed in a public epilogue is evidence of the strain under

which he was labouring. How great this was, is only too clear in his letters:

> Could I see you without passion [he wrote] or be absent from you without pain, I need not beg your pardon for this renewing my vows, that I love you more than health or any happiness here, or hereafter. Everything you do is a new charm to me; and though I have languished for seven long tedious years of desire, jealously despairing; yet every minute I see you, I still discover something new and more bewitching... Give me a word or two of comfort, or resolve never to look with common goodness on me more, for I cannot bear a kind look, and after it a cruel denial. This minute my heart aches for you: and if I cannot have a right in yours, I wish it would ache till I could complain to you no longer.
>
> *Remember poor* Otway.

This sounds curiously in a Restoration figure; here is no attempt to rationalize love, nor to seek an easy physical equivalent. It is nearer to Julie de Lespinasse:

> Les troubles et l'agitation de mes idées et de mon âme m'ont privée longtemps de l'usage de mes facultés. J'éprouvais ce que dit Rousseau, qu'il y a des situations qui n'ont ni mots ni larmes. J'ai passé huit jours dans les convulsions du désespoir: j'ai cru mourir, je voulais mourir, et cela me paraissait plus aisé que de renoncer à vous aimer.

It was for this emotion, with its parallel outlook on life, that Otway sought body in his tragedies.

A victim of unrequited love, he palpably relied upon the expression of the tortures of love for his most poignant scenes. 'His inimitable·skill in representing the motions of the heart and its affections', his editor of 1757 wrote, 'is such that the circumstances are great from the art of the poet, rather than from the fortunes of the persons represented.' If the phrase is in itself an adverse criticism, since the emotions should not outgrow the fortunes of the persons (that being sentimentality), it is at least an accurate

one. Dryden also, not very well disposed towards Otway,
commended him highly for his treatment of the passions :
and perhaps as great a tribute as any came from Mrs. Barry
herself, who confessed that she could never utter in *The
Orphan* the words ' Ah! poor Castalia!' without dropping
a tear.

There is, indeed, rather too much of the tearful element
in Otway—we might almost say of tear-mongering. His
sentimentality is not confined to love, and he may be
accused of having opened the door to the worst kind of
maudlin whimpering which was later to distinguish popular
melodrama, namely, the heart-wringing operated by the
' little chee-ild '.

Caius Marius. Take hence this brat too ; mount it on a spear,
   And make it sprawl to make the grandsire sport.
Child. O cruel man! I'll hang upon your knees,
   And with my little dying hands implore you :
   I may be fit to do you some small pleasures.
   I'll find a thousand tender ways to please you :
   Smile when you rage, and stroke you into mildness ;
   Play with your manly neck, and call you father :
   For mine (alas!) the Gods have taken from me.
          (*Caius Marius*, v. iii.)

The Elizabethans sometimes had recourse to the child to
make the lump rise in the throat ; but we have only to
compare that passage with Arthur pleading for his eyes in
King John, or the picture of Giovanni in *The White Devil*,
to see how far away Otway was from the sense of life of
the Elizabethans.

The two most important of his tragedies are *The Orphan*
and *Venice Preserv'd*, for *Caius Marius* is not on the same
poetic level, in spite of its copious borrowings from *Romeo
and Juliet*, ' improved ', it need hardly be said, to suit the
theories and taste of the time. Yet it had been well if some-

thing of the virile quality which appears in it, and which he was able to maintain when away from the distresses of Mrs. Barry's fast and loose behaviour, had stiffened the structure of the other plays, which depend too much upon piteous love even for their sort, and not enough upon admiration. 'Tender Otway !'—the epithet rises almost inevitably to the lips upon reading *The Orphan*, which is the most Racinian of his tragedies, not because he approaches nearer the French in form, but because on certain sides the development of his sensibility seems to correspond with that of Racine. In the sort of emotion which this play contains he is almost unmatchable ; almost, because Ford still overtops him. Although less really concerned with death than the Jacobeans, for whom the constant plagues provided such irresistible wealth of charnel-house imagery, yet it is in connexion with death that he achieves his most memorably tender effects. Listen to Monimia :

> When I'm laid low i'the grave, and quite forgotten,
> May'st thou be happy in a fairer bride ;
> But none can ever love thee like Monimia.
> When I am dead, as presently I shall be
> (For the grim Tyrant grasps my heart already),
> Speak well of me ; and if thou find ill tongues
> Too busy with my fame, don't hear me wronged ;
> 'Twill be a noble justice to the memory
> Of a poor wretch once honoured with thy love.
> How my head swims ! 'Tis very dark. Good-night. (*Dies.*)
>
> (v. i.)

It is, of course, full of echoes, enriched by memories of Fletcher, Webster, and others, and it is just by comparisons with the earlier work that Otway's poetic weakness reveals itself. The charge of plagiarism frequently brought against him would not matter, certainly as regards plot, where he was not inventive, were it not for the continual enfeeble-

ment of the idea. When Brachiano is violently upbraiding
Vittoria, he cries:

> Thou hast led me like a heathen sacrifice,
> With music and with fatal yoke of flowers,
> To mine eternal ruin,

but Otway, with a reminiscence perhaps of O *fons Ban-
dusiae*, expands it in *Venice Preserv'd* to:

> Come, lead me forward now like a tame lamb
> To sacrifice ; thus in his fatal garlands
> Decked fine, and pleased, the wanton skips and plays,
> Trots by the enticing flattering priestess' side,
> And, much transported with its little pride,
> Forgets his dear companions of the plain ;
> Till by her bound he's on the altar lain,
> Yet then he hardly bleats, such pleasure's in the pain.

> (IV. i.)

The falsity in the last line is evident, but throughout there is
a sentimental relaxation : the images of the lamb are better
to draw a maiden's tears than to ring the tragic note.
What was always happening with Otway is clear from another comparison. When, in *The Revenge of Bussy d'Ambois*,
Guise apprehends a speedy death, he says:

> 'You're a dead man if you enter' ;
> And these words this imperfect blood and flesh
> Shrink at in spite of me, their solidest part
> Melting like snow within me with cold fire :
> I hate myself, that seeking to rule kings
> I cannot curb my slave.

Now this is Otway in *Don Carlos*:

> What's all my glory, all my pomp ? How poor
> Is fading greatness ! or how vain is power !
> Where all the mighty conquests I have seen ?
> I, who o'er other nations have victorious been,
> Now cannot quell one little foe within,

but here the enemy within is not the fear of death, but,

characteristically, jealousy! Thus although hopeless love may have made Otway a poet, it miserably reduced the scale of his conceptions, for he could not rid himself of his haunting idea.

If the fable of *The Orphan* is more fit to bear the treatment Otway was able to give a tragedy, *Venice Preserv'd*, grandiose and sombre in design, is continually marred by his preoccupation with his personal troubles. The theme of unfortunate love bulks far too large in it, and though Belvidera supplies a necessary element, one cannot always refrain from wishing her away. Being familiar with the atmosphere of fell designs, the Popish Plot still occupying the minds of men, Otway raises against the smoky background of sinister plotters, suspicious friends, and would-be Romans, a stark tragedy of personal friendship, betrayal, and consequent remorse and expiation. Even those hideously masochistic scenes of Antonio, virulent satire against Shaftesbury, serve his purpose as 'the last twist of the knife', and cannot be omitted; and though the play is unrelieved by any element of strong sanity—for like himself, perhaps, all his characters are 'too unhappy to be good'—it might have been a tragedy of the first order. As it is, softened throughout by the very eighteenth-century romantic love, incongruous with the other more Elizabethan elements, it must rank well below *All for Love* in sustained interest. Dryden, as he said, would have liked to work up the love-pity to a greater height, but was denied this owing to the 'crimes of love' of his protagonists, but in Otway's play there is too much. There, the necessary pity, as well as the something nearer to admiration than terror, is already in Pierre and Jaffeir, so that the insistence upon the piteous in Belvidera topples the tragedy too far over into mournful contemplation. Indeed, Belvidera's preliminary 'distraction' scene was deservedly made fun of some twenty-five years later by Gay, in *The What D'ye Call It*.

One cannot but feel that in this play Otway was concerned, not with a tragic vision, nor with the delineation of character, but with the emotions as such. He was exploring not man's courage so much as his capacity for feeling, even for self-torture. Jaffeir's remorse and self-abasement are terrible to listen to; Otway seems to be indulging in a debauch of his own pains. The dignity of the play resides almost wholly in Pierre, about whom there really is something fine, but even he is too intent upon his feelings:

Pierre. Come, where's my dungeon? lead me to my straw:
　　It will not be the first time I've lodged hard
　　To do your Senate service.
Jaffeir. 　　　　　　　　Hold one moment.
Pierre. Who's he disputes the judgment of the Senate?
　　Presumptuous rebel —— on —— 　　(*Strikes* Jaff.)
Jaffeir. 　　　　　　　By Heaven you stir not.
　　I must be heard, I must have leave to speak:
　　Thou hast disgraced me, Pierre, by a vile blow:
　　Had not a dagger done thee nobler justice?
　　But use me as thou wilt, thou can'st not wrong me,
　　For I am fall'n beneath the basest injuries;
　　Yet look upon me with an eye of mercy,
　　With pity and with charity behold me;
　　Shut not your heart against a friend's repentance,
　　But as there dwells a God-like nature in thee,
　　Listen with mildness to my supplications.
Pierre. What whining monk art thou? what holy cheat,
　　That would'st encroach upon my credulous ears,
　　And cant'st thus vilely? Hence. I know thee not.
　　Dissemble and be nasty: leave me, hypocrite!
Jaffeir. Not know me, Pierre!
Pierre. No, I know thee not: what art thou?
Jaffeir. Jaffeir, thy friend, thy once loved, valued friend!
　　Though now deserv'dly scorned, and used most hardly.
Pierre. Thou Jaffeir! thou my once lov'd, valued friend!

By Heaven thou liest; the man so called, my friend,
Was generous, honest, faithful, just and valiant,
Noble in mind, and in his person lovely,
Dear to my eyes, and tender to my heart:
But thou, a wretched, base, false, worthless coward,
Poor, even in soul, and loathsome in thy aspect:
All eyes must shun thee, and all hearts detest thee.
Prithee avoid, nor longer cling thus round me
Like something baneful, that my nature's chilled at.

Jaffeir. I have not wronged thee, by these tears I have not.
But still am honest, true, and hope too, valiant;
My mind still full of thee: therefore still noble,
Let not thy eyes then shun me, nor thy heart
Detest me utterly: Oh look upon me,
Look back and see my sad, sincere submission!
How my heart swells, as even 'twould burst my bosom;
Fond of its goal, and labouring to be at thee!
What shall I do? what say to make thee hear me?

Pierre. Hast thou not wronged me? dar'st thou call thyself,
That once loved, honest, valued friend of mine,
And swear thou hast not wronged me? Whence these
chains?
Whence the vile death, which I may meet this moment?
Whence this dishonour, but from thee, thou false one?

Jaffeir. All's true, yet grant one thing, and I've done asking.

Pierre. What's that?

Jaffeir.   To take thy life on such conditions
The Council have proposed. Thou and thy friends
May yet live long, and to be better treated.

Pierre. Life! ask my life! Confess! Record myself
A villain for the privilege to breathe,
And carry up and down this cursed city
A discontented and repining spirit,
Burdensome to itself, a few years longer,
To lose, it may be, at last in a lewd quarrel
For some new friend, treacherous and false as thou art!
No, this vile world and I have long been jangling,
And cannot part on better terms than now,
When only men like thee are fit to live in't.

Jaffeir. By all that's just——

Pierre.   Swear by some other powers,
For thou hast broke that sacred oath too lately.

Jaffeir.	Then by that hell I merit, I'll not leave thee
	Till to thyself at least thou'rt reconciled ;
	However thy resentments deal with me.
Pierre.	Not leave me !
Jaffeir.	No ; thou shalt not force me from thee :
	Use me reproachfully, and like a slave ;
	Tread on me, buffet me, heap wrongs on wrongs
	On my poor head ; I'll bear it all with patience,
	Shall weary out thy most unfriendly cruelty :
	Lie at thy feet and kiss 'em, though they spurn me,
	Till wounded by my sufferings you relent,
	And raise me to thy arms with dear forgiveness.
Pierre.	Art thou not——
Jaffeir.	What ?
Pierre.	A traitor ?
Jaffeir.	Yes.
Pierre.	A villain ?
Jaffeir.	Granted.
Pierre.	A coward, a most scandalous coward,
	Spiritless, void of honour, one who has sold
	Thy everlasting fame for shameless life ?
Jaffeir.	All, all, and more, much more ; my faults are number-
	less. (IV. ii.)

One thing, and one thing only, could have saved this play—a higher poetic potential. The verse is too diffuse. It is true that there is none of the fantastic imagery, none of the ranting of Lee ; but ranting sometimes introduces a bonier element than Otway was able to supply. He lacked the power to concentrate much feeling in a phrase, the gift of compelling imagery upon which the imagination can feed, that rapid connexion of ideas of which some of the Eliza-bethans were such great masters. There is none of those unforgettably vivid sentences shot out swiftly to define a phase, like lightning showing up the murk. He was rightly praised for the naturalness of his diction, but the simple statement, if it is to be moving and revealing, requires a great and complicated preparation, and a weight of feeling which will not endure the least alloy of sentimentality. Restraint and simplicity are not foundations upon which dramatic poems of this kind can be built: they are the pinnacle. Think of the ornament on the one hand, and the passion on the other, required to make effective such things as Macduff's ' He has no children ', or Phèdre's ' Ils s'aimeront toujours!' Otway's very naturalness led him astray; and thus, at the critical moments, passages which might tell through a sublime simplicity have to be replaced by speeches which appear forced in the setting provided for them. For although the play moves in its atmosphere of distorted passions well enough to bear almost any weight of poetic tension, his pity-mongering on behalf of love undermines the emotional structure, and he would have done well to remember his earliest master's injunctions in the preface to *Mithridate*, where he declared that ' les plus belles scènes sont en danger d' ennuyer du moment qu' on peut les séparer de l' action, et qu'elles l' interrompent au lieu de la conduire vers sa fin '. Yet it would be ungrateful to deny him those shining qualities he had, that reality of passion in which he exceeded nearly all (one might well risk all) his contemporaries. For his genius was of an order of which we can forgive the immaturities, and if ever our national theatre takes form, *Venice Preserv'd* must certainly be second on the list of Restoration tragedies. He was only thirty-three when he died, and had he lived he might have found a mould for his own peculiar sense of fact, and disciplined the latter into material for art. Unfitted to excel his fellows within the dramatic limits the critics of his age had evolved—he had already burst the form—it was a sign of originality in him to break back to a previous age. It was, perhaps, a preliminary to forging forward into the new age of English tragic drama which has yet to come.

VIII

NICHOLAS ROWE (1674–1718)

The Ambitious Stepmother, 1700.
Tamerlane, 1701.
The Fair Penitent, 1703.
Ulysses, 1705.
The Royal Convert, 1707.
Jane Shore, 1714.
Lady Jane Gray, 1715.

Do you remember *Approchez-vous, Néron*—who would not rather have thought of that half-line than all Mr. Rowe's flowers of eloquence?

Gray to Walpole, Jan. 1747.

GRAY'S remark might be all that it is necessary to say about Rowe, were it not that the distinction between his prettiness and that of Dryden must be made, and that under his guidance we see tragedy, as Mr. Elwin has stressed in his recent *Handbook to Restoration Drama*, deserting its old realm, and making rapid strides towards domestic tragedy.

Rowe's prettiness consists in what, in his dedication of *Lady Jane Gray*, he called 'poetic colouring'—that is to say, not in structure, in the swaying backwards and forwards of the emotions, nor indeed in any final vision, but in words which he thought, according to a theory of poetry more persistent among idle laymen than among poets, were beautiful, charming, soothing. There were certain groups of ideas, of images, and naturally of words, which could be expected to do the trick. What exactly the trick was it might be hard to define, but it was the sort of thing well-brought-up people would recognize at once. With Rowe we are well into the eighteenth century. Gray might not think very highly of Rowe, but the latter would have agreed that the language of poetry was not that of every day. Unfortunately, the language of drama, at its most tense moments, is never anything else. *Approchez-vous, Néron!* The drama may be, indeed it certainly is, dramatic poesy; but it relies on rather different elements from those which poetry takes for its uses when meant only to be read. Confusing the two lent a certain air of sentimentality to Rowe's work: yet we must beware of using the word 'sentimentality', for it is an epithet we are apt to apply to sets of emotions which other people feel, but which we do not happen to share.

Nevertheless it would be absurd to credit Rowe with any real tragic sense. He was somewhat confused in his mind as to what tragedy was expected to do, as is proper to a man who was incurably gay, much to Addison's displeasure, and spent his days in bed and his nights out of it. There is, of course, no reason why a light heart and tragedy should not go together, as much as a heavy one with comedy, but the heart must hanker after solitude rather than after the Kit-Cat. Such a heart as Rowe's could feel pity, but could not face the terror of tragedy. His poetic justice, as stated in the Epistle Dedicatory of his first play, is too easy; the 'principal contrivers of evil' are punished with death. And though in his last play the conception was modified, the Catonic sublimity of the good people's death is well worth the triumph of the unscrupulous survivors. At all events pity must have the last word. The audience 'should be struck with terror in several parts of the play, but always conclude and go away with pity, a sort of regret proceeding from good-nature which, though an uneasiness, is not altogether disagreeable to the person who feels it'. This is not quite the same as the evaporation of all disagreeables, which Keats regarded as the test of tragedy, for in Rowe there is none of the fire which could produce enough heat to make anything evaporate. It is all very smooth and gentleman-like: it must appeal, as his eighteenth-century editress said, to all persons of taste; unluckily taste is a variable fashion. Rowe did make something, but what he made was eighteenth-century frontispiece illustrations to the plays of Shakespeare—or of any one else. The composition is urbane, the persons represented well recognizable as embodying something, the gestures neo-classic, the drapery correct. Some people collect such engravings. Thus it is no shame to enjoy the plays of Rowe, so long as one does not confuse that pleasure with the quite different emotions of tragedy. His works are, as Smollett remarked, solid, florid, declamatory: solidity is no mean achievement.

We easily lose sight of the solidity of his plays in their floridness. It is not quite true that, as Dr. Johnson remarked, ' he always delights the ear and often improves the under-standing ', for he never does the latter, and ' soothes ' would be a better word than ' delights '. But his morals are im-peccable, if that was what Dr. Johnson meant. His favour-ites display every acknowledged virtue, his sinners leave no doubt about their vice: there is no inner struggle worth considering. But all this is very much to the good. The indubitable values make up the eighteenth-century solidity, about which the declamatory ornaments can safely be hung. Only in *The Fair Penitent* is there any of the turbulence or trouble of real drama, and this was not his favourite play, though it is that of present posterity. We are not so con-scious of ' poetic beauties ', as we read it; these are to be found more abundantly in other plays, which breathe an air, if not of serenity, at least of decorous melancholy.

Mention has been made of settled values, and the term was used to mean more normal values, rather than the artificial ones of heroic tragedy proper: the setting was gone, and the brilliant lighting went with it. There are, as one would imagine, echoes of the world which disappeared with the Act of Settlement: for instance, the stage was not yet rid of Rome. Thus Sciolto in *The Fair Penitent* will see justice executed, 'even to a Roman strictness'; Lady Jane Gray, with a change of view as to Roman characteristics which may have been due to Addison's *Cato* (like Cato, she consults the Platonic dialogues to assure herself of her soul, although a model Christian), suggests to her friends that they should greet their enemies calmly, and 'stand unmoved; as once the Roman Senate received fierce Brennus'. Rowe was on fairly safe ground there, but his attitude to the old heroic values is doubtful. His first play, *The Ambitious Stepmother*, seems the most definite, and we read

> Ambition! the desire of active souls,
> That pushes 'em beyond the bounds of nature.

But that is only a flicker of the old grand manner: it is, in tone, completely unlike the Machiavellian Empress of Morocco's

> A statesman's breast should scorn to feel remorse;
> Murder and treason are but things of course.

At the later date the figures do not move outside humane possibilities; there are no glorious orgies of heroic slaying. According to Rowe there is still a certain amount to be said for heroic greatness, the greatness of kings after the model of his idol, William III—of kings, that is, who take their responsibilities seriously; but love, instead of being an added glory, has become a danger. Tamerlane struggles against it; he will not lose a friend 'poorly for a woman', yet later is forced to confess:

> One moment more, and I too late shall find
> That love's the strongest pow'r that lords it o'er the mind.

Antinous in *Ulysses* says of himself:

> Think not I dream the hours of life away,
> Supine, and negligent of love and glory,

as though the two things were naturally linked together. Yet a minute later he finds that love in his rival is a 'convenient dotage':

> Youth by nature
> Is active, fiery, bold, and great of soul;
> Love is the bane of all these noble qualities,
> The sickly fit that kills ambition's appetite.

Love has, in fact, become a 'softer thought'. One of the main props of heroic tragedy has collapsed, and Rowe even resents any attempt of his characters to revive it. When the king in *The Royal Convert* says:

> Each minute shall be rich in some great action,
> To speak the king, the hero and the lover.

Seofrid rebukes him with:

> The hero and the king are glorious names,
> But oh! my master, wherefore is the lover?

Rowe, apparently, had a shrewd suspicion that heroic love, with its devastating suddenness, deserved to be called something else. It was certainly Seofrid's Platonic opinion:

> And love, or call it by the coarser name,
> Lust, is, of all the frailties of our nature,
> What most we ought to fear; the headstrong heart
> Rushes along, impatient of the course,
> Nor hears the rider's call, nor feels the rein.

Love, indeed, to conclude upon this point, was apt to be a

little namby-pamby, and this view is amusingly stated by the Machiavellian Mirza in *The Ambitious Stepmother*:

> Love! what is love? the passion of a boy
> That spends his time in laziness and sonnets:
> Lust is the appetite of man;

with which Napoleonic sentiment we may leave illustration.

Love, obviously, exists in Rowe's plays, but it is not heroic love; it is something much truer to life—it is domestic love on a fairly high level, with implications to be discussed later. But so long as the general framework remained heroic, something had to be substituted for the old kind of love, and this is where 'poetic beauties' take their turn. They become almost the object of the plays, and do not take their place as a sort of cement to the structure, as they do with Dryden. On occasion they intrude ruinously. When Jane Shore, redeemed by misfortune from her courtesan life, is found and reclaimed by her husband, she, who now understands the beauty of domestic affection, cries out, as she remembers Shore's 'diligence of love':

> Have you forgot
> The costly string of pearls you brought me home
> And tied about my neck? How could I leave you?

merely because it was time some rich image was introduced. When she faints, and Shore revives her with a stimulant, he has to say:

> She faints! support her!
> Sustain her head while I infuse this cordial
> Into her dying lips—from spicy drugs,
> Rich herbs and flow'rs, the potent juice is drawn;
> With wondrous force it strikes the lazy spirits,
> Drives 'em around, and wakens life anew.   (v. i.)

The innocence, the beauty, the freshness of flowers, these are more poetic, more true to nature, than pearls, which

are a trifle exotic; they remind us of Marlowe, rather than
of those purer models, Shakespeare and Fletcher. The set
of counters which goes to make up the poetic pattern is
becoming more limited. Thus Guilford, in *Lady Jane
Gray*:

> Thou weep'st, my queen, and hang'st thy drooping head,
> Like nodding poppies, heavy with the rain,
> That bow their weary necks, and bend to earth.

And Ethelinda in *The Royal Convert* (Act IV):

> Oh, my love!
> What can I pay thee back for all this truth?
> What! but, like thee, to triumph in my fate,
> And think it more than life to die with thee.
> Haste then, ye virgins, break the tender turf,
> And let your chaster hands prepare the bed,
> Where my dear lord and I must rest together;
> Then let the myrtle and the rose be strowed,
> For 'tis my second better bridal day.
> On my cold bosom let his head be laid,
> And look that none disturb us,
> Till the last trumpet's sound break our long sleep,
> And calls us to the everlasting bliss.   (i. i.)

And Axalla in *Tamerlane*:

> The murmuring gale revives the drooping flame,
> That at thy coldness languished in my breast;
> So breathe the gentle zephyrs on the Spring,
> And waken every plant, and od'rous flower
> Which winter frost had blasted, to new life.

Indeed one must at this point confess, with the best will
in the world not to abuse the term, that Rowe's work is
sentimental; there is no reality of emotion corresponding
with the sets of ideas offered: it has not even the hardness
real artificiality can give, as it does to the pastorals of
Pope. Take this from Telemachus to Semanthe, in *Ulysses*:

> It shall be so,—I will be faithful to thee,
> For days, for months, for years I will be miserable,

> Protract my suff'rings ev'n to hoary age,
> And linger out a tedious life in pain;
> In spite of sickness and a broken heart,
> I will endure for ages to obey thee.   (v. i.)

Finally, there is the 'never . . . more' combination, which runs like a refrain through a large part of Restoration tragedy, always with a strongly emotive intent. When all else fails, that is a sure counter to play. With Lee, who uses it a good deal, it becomes absorbed in the general rush and grandiosity; with Rowe it stands out, though he does not resort to it nearly so often as Lee. Yet in *Jane Shore* the emotive gong sounds a little too often:

> For thou shalt never never part us more,

we read; and three pages on, in rapid succession:

> Would I had ne'er survived to see thee more. . .
> And let 'em never vex thy quiet more.

Nevertheless, the sense of finality is lacking.

Yet it is well that Rowe should have been content to write this dulcet stuff, with pretty little experiments in metre here and there, with rhymes to mark an effective exit, or to usher out the act with muted music. His attempts to write a little closer to the heroic plan often end in bathos, such as the superbly droll remark of Calista in *The Fair Penitent*:

> Is it the voice of thunder, or my father?

a doubt which even distraction could hardly excuse. He occasionally tried to stiffen the matter with generalities, with speeches of philosophical or political import—for after all he was Shakespeare's first editor. Thus Hastings in *Jane Shore* (III. i):

> The resty knaves are overrun with ease,
> As plenty ever is the nurse of faction:
> If in good days, like these, the headstrong herd

Grow madly wanton and repine; it is
Because the reins of power are held too slack,
And reverend authority of late
Has worn a face of mercy more than justice.

It would be cruel to print a passage from Dryden, still more so one from Shakespeare, to mark the difference between what will do and what will not: the obvious thing about this one is, not so much that the thought is inadequate or trite, as that it has not occurred to Rowe with the force of an original discovery, nor has the verse itself the vigour to make it seem as though it had. Rowe was not built to see things on the tragic scale: even in his plays of larger scope it is the domestic side which he works out with most enthusiasm and with most skill, a fact which calls for some comment.

For the question which sooner or later must be asked is whether the phrase 'domestic tragedy' is not in itself a contradiction in terms? Is not the truth of such a form of drama inevitably a 'yesterday truth', a local truth? Of course, on any theory of tragedy which asks merely for the emotions to be aroused, for a state of sensibility to be induced in an audience luxuriating in its sorrow, the question does not arise. There, the sad death from consumption of Mr. Bun the Baker is every whit as much a tragic theme as that of Macbeth from quite different causes; the fate of Tchekov's three sisters provides as valuable a subject for an 'im tation of life' as the fate of the daughters of Œdipus or Lear: whether the one can be made as catholic as the other the future has yet to decide.

It is probable that scarcely anybody to-day holds the old rigid theory that tragedies are the sad stories of the deaths of kings; our conception has widened, whatever may have happened to its depth. The definition suggested earlier in this book is, that it is the vision of some magnificent person or fine thing (which is much the same) shattered by something less admirable, though perhaps more useful: it mirrors life in a universal way because the story deals, not with characters or individuals for their own sake, but with the sort of thing which happens to mankind, and which mankind has to harden itself against. There is no *a priori* reason why domestic tragedy should not conform to such a definition just as much as classical and Shakespearian tragedy. It may be harder to arrive at the sense of universality, of the thing mattering; but this will depend upon what the writers can bring to the theme. It would be folly to deny that Ibsen did accomplish something very like classical tragedy in *The Master Builder*; or that Mr. Granville Barker approaches near to it in *Waste*. But in the first we are too conscious of symbolism; in the second we are invited to consider a moral question. The problem play can never be a great play, because a work of art neither asks questions nor answers them: it states the facts the writer has discovered, and states them for their own sake.

Distressing, then, as it may seem, tragedy is a spectacle— a spectacle which unsentimentalizes man, and tests his endurance of life. It also confirms his common knowledge that that is how things happen, and that death is the end of all. This may seem too simple, but it involves a great deal; for the one spectacle which can certainly perform the work in men's emotions and attitudes which we expect tragedy to perform is the spectacle of the Dying God.* It is doubtful if man will ever free himself from his ancestry of believers in magic, or from the fascination of blood: to

---

* The connexion of the Dying God with Shakespearian tragedy was made by Mr. Wyndham Lewis in his brilliant *The Lion and the Fox*.

watch anything struggling against death has the allurement of the terrible. This can perhaps be provided in some degree by domestic tragedy, but it is only in the god dying that the something else we need, and are satisfied of in earlier tragedy, can be found. Thus Sir J. G. Frazer writes: 'The accumulated misfortunes and sins of the whole people are sometimes laid upon the dying god, who is supposed to bear them away for ever, leaving the people innocent and happy.' He adds: 'The notion that we can transfer our guilt and sufferings to some other being who will bear them for us is familiar to the savage mind': and he might have said further, practically ineradicable from the civilized one, where the mass is concerned. Our difficulty is that, though we often manage to shift the guilt, as the nations have universally done as regards the last war, we often have to endure the sufferings, though on a small scale the scapegoat is a common figure enough. These feelings, it need hardly be said, are submerged and disguised in a civilized community, or are absorbed into religion; nevertheless the desire remains for the sort of spectacle referred to.

How far it is tragic would seem to depend upon how far the things we consider essential in life are involved. Originally, everything essential to life depended on the *death* of the god; but as soon as mankind passed beyond the fertility ritual, it was the fact that so much depended on the *life* of the god (who was then reduced to the scale of king) that made the spectacle absorbing; thus it was only so long as the person of the king remained of prime importance in the state that to be a tragic figure was a royal prerogative. Rowe came to write after the Revolution; George Barnwell represents the House of Hanover as significantly as George I does, and goes further towards democracy. The tragic figure, then, can no longer stand for

mankind, or for a nation: no more can one country, or a third
of the world, cry to another country, ' I'm dying, Egypt,
dying!' It is extremely hard to replace this sentiment of
greatness by any symbolism whatever in domestic tragedy.
Strindberg, perhaps, gets closer than any other playwright
in such plays as *The Dance of Death*, or in *The Father*, which
is the same sort of thing, adapted to modern life, as *King
Lear*. Other writers only replace it by poignancy, that of
Rosmersholm, or *Uncle Vanya*. But the part of the spectacle
of the god dying is lost: the issues may be as important to
us, if we can really feel ourselves involved, but part of the
emotive element in tragedy is precisely in the death of a
noble beast, because there we see the eternal struggle of life
against death. It is this, and not sadism, which keeps the
bull-fight alive. The humanitarian who sees in it nothing
but a foolish animal put to torture turns away in disgust;
but the less encumbered person, who sees in the animal a
symbol of strength and life, is bound to feel a fascination
in watching its death throes. This is tragedy at its crudest;
but it is one of the elements which make *Œdipus*, *Ajax*,
Othello, *Lear*, and so on, tragic. The god who has to die
must be as well a large, sacrificial beast: there is no tragedy
in the death of a louse, whereas pity and fear are present
in the death lashings of any powerful brute. The small
beast can evoke pity, but not terror: and terror, it would
seem, is the element which gives the sense of universality
to a tragedy. Or, to put it differently, since sensitiveness
has replaced power as the thing to be destroyed, terror has
disappeared—which may be the reason that makes *Hamlet*
so puzzling, and, to many, so unsatisfying a tragedy; for
it is a tragedy of sensitiveness worked out as a tragedy of
power.

So far, there can be no doubt, domestic tragedy has not

succeeded in conveying the same emotions as tragedy proper, except, vaguely, when it has ceased to be domestic strictly speaking, and has become symbolic, a way trodden to the extreme point by the Expressionists. All drama, naturally, is symbolic, but royal tragedy assumes that the symbol chosen, namely royalty, is the best for its purpose: domestic tragedy seems all the time to be trying to make the best of a symbol thrust upon it, and to be making it bear more than it properly can. Thus the symbol remains symbol instead of becoming life. This is true only of stage tragedy: in the novel matters appear to be different, per-haps because there the same concentration is not necessary, and that a slow development will enable feelings to be built up on a domestic level, while the necessary rapidity of the drama demands adventitious aid in the form of some accepted symbol, which will in five minutes do the work it may take the novel five long chapters to perform. Maybe Mr. C. K. Munro's plays are the nearest approach to tragedy written in Europe since the rise of constitutional govern-ment, because there the figure of the king is replaced by some political idea.

It has been suggested earlier that poignancy is appealed to in this sort of tragedy to make up for the absence of universality; and this certainly is what Rowe aimed at from the very first, as is plain from his prologue to *The Ambitious Stepmother*:

> If dying lovers yet deserve a tear,
> If a sad story of a maid's despair
> Yet move compassion in the pitying fair...

he begins, to acknowledge a debt to Otway a few lines lower down; for the tears of the fair, he says,

> ... did moving Otway's labours crown,
> And make the poor Monimia's griefs their own,

the tragic muse having evidently forestalled Addison's philosophy in frequenting the tea-table. A dying lover is not a dying god, but it was the lover in the man, whether he were a king or not, that interested Rowe. His domestic tragedy is something quite different from Racine's, for with Racine the lover and the king struggle together in the same person; the lover may be one of the king's destroyers, which fact keeps Racine's plays within the frame of tragedy proper: with Rowe, the lover happens to be a king, or the king happens to be a lover, but no figure is convincingly both at one and the same time. Although his plays still have sufficiently grandiose titles and personages, with the exception of *Jane Shore*, which is frankly domestic, and, of course, of *The Fair Penitent*, we are not intended to be concerned at the variations of their 'great fortunes'. Chaucer stated that:

> Tragedie is noon oother maner thyng,
> Ne kan in syngyng crie ne biwaille,
> But that Fortune alwey wole assaille
> With unwar strook the regnes that been proude;
> For whan men trusteth hire, thanne wol she faille
> And covere hire brighte face with a clowde:

but it is doubtful if Rowe would have done the statement more than lip service. What he was after was not an expression of the dreadful workings of fate, but the agreeable workings of the domestic emotions, and what might to-day be called the bourgeois (that is, the certainly comfortable and perhaps necessary) virtues. He might feign to be presenting 'regnes that been proude', and so on, but his real counters, the things he most depended on for his effects, were the feelings with which the readers of *The Spectator* were familiar.

The influence of Otway, or at least of *The Orphan*, is

undoubted, yet it is difficult to regard Otway as the precursor of George Lillo, for one feels that he is returning to Ford rather than trying to adventure in a new realm; and in this respect one may possibly admit his return to the Elizabethans, remembering always his different sensibility. But Ford's tragedy is not domestic, as we have come to use the word, because the feelings are raised to a height of passion which takes them out of the domestic region. Rowe, if he returns to anything, goes back to *The Yorkshire Tragedy* and *Arden of Feversham*, but those strange plays should, for safety's sake, be left out of any genealogy, whereas a claim might be made for Heywood's *A Woman Killed with Kindness*. The point really is, that with Otway, just as with Ford, there is the background of fear: a larger conception is, if not stated, at least implied. There is a faint echo of it in *The Fair Penitent*, but it is absent from the rest of the plays of the man who crowned a successful career by becoming Under-Secretary of State as well as Poet Laureate.

The remark is no mere gibe: a man may be an excellent civil servant and a good poet—there is M. Paul Claudel to prove it—but Rowe's plays grew more polite and less dramatic as time went on. His promise of exploring a new region of sensibility was never fulfilled. He improved in diction and versification; his blank verse became more flexible, and lost the sense, which we noted in Addison's verse but which was never so strongly marked as in Addison's, of being made up of rhymed verses with the rhymes taken out. But his diction, though good, never pierces, nor does it attain the organ sonority of Ford. One of his best scenes, however, is in his last play. There is a certain dramatic movement in the reconciliation between Pembroke and Guilford, and it happens to be almost the only scene free of extraneous poetic beauties. Pembroke, who was Guilford's bosom friend, but who broke with him and joined Mary's party when Guilford married Lady Jane Gray, with whom he was himself passionately in love, is being led off to prison. Guilford comes in:

Guilford. Is all the gentleness that was betwixt us
So lost, so swept away from thy remembrance,
Thou can'st not look upon me?

Pembroke.   Ha! not look!
What terrors are there in the Dudley's race,
That Pembroke dares not look upon, and scorn?
And yet, 'tis true, I would not look upon thee;
Our eyes avoid to look on what we hate,
As well as what we fear.

Guilford.   You hate me then!

Pembroke. I do; and wish perdition may o'ertake
Thy father, thy false self, and thy whole name.

Guilford. And yet, as sure as rage disturbs thy reason,
And masters all the noble nature in thee,
As sure as thou hast wronged me, I am come
In tenderness of friendship to preserve thee;
To plant ev'n all the power I have before thee,
And fence thee from destruction with my life.

Pembroke. Friendship from thee! But my just soul disdains thee!
Hence! take the prostituted bauble back,
Hang it to grace some slavering idiot's neck,
For none but fools will prize the tinsel toy.
But thou art come, perhaps, to vaunt thy greatness,
To set thy purple pomp to view before me;
To let me know that Guilford is a king,
That he can speak the word, and give me freedom.
Oh! Short-lived pageant! Had'st thou all the pow'r
Which thy vain soul would grasp at I would die,
Rot in a dungeon, ere receive a grace,
The least, the meanest courtesy from thee.

Guilford. Oh, Pembroke! But I have not time to talk,
For danger presses, danger unforeseen,
As secret as the shaft that flies by night,
Is aiming at thy life. Captain, a word!
                                        (*To the Officer.*)
I take your prisoner to my proper charge;

Draw off your guard, and leave his sword with me.
(*The officer delivers the sword, and draws off:*
Guilford offers the sword to Pembroke.)
Receive this gift, ev'n from a rival's hand;
And if thy rage will suffer thee to hear
The counsel of a man once called thy friend
Fly from this fatal place, and seek thy safety.

Pembroke. How now! What show? What mockery is this?
Is it in sport you use me thus? What means
This swift fantastic changing of the scene?

Guilford. Oh! take thy sword; and let thy valiant hand
Be ready armed to guard thy noble life:
The time, the danger, and thy wild impatience
Forbid me all to enter into speech with thee,
Or I could tell thee—

Pembroke.   No, it needs not, traitor;
For all thy poor, thy little arts are known.
Thou fear'st my vengeance, and art come to fawn,
To make a merit of that proffered freedom,
Which, in despite of thee, a day shall give me.
Nor can my fate depend on thee, false Guilford;
For, know to thy confusion, ere the sun
Twice gild the East, our royal Mary comes
To end thy pageant reign and set me free.

Guilford. Ungrateful and unjust! hast thou known me
So little, to accuse my heart of fear?
Hast thou forgotten Musselborough's field?
Did I then fear, when by thy side I fought,
And dyed my maiden sword in Scottish blood?
But this is madness all!

Pembroke.   Give me my sword.
Perhaps indeed I wrong thee. (IV. i.)

He is prepared at this point to fight an honourable duel
with Guilford; but the latter, after as much talk again,
and the production of documentary evidence, proves to
Pembroke that if he stays he will be murdered. At last,
convinced of his friend's good faith, Pembroke 'sees his
honest heart' and his own peril.

Guilford. Waste not the time. Away!
Pembroke.   Here let me fix,
And gaze with everlasting wonder on thee.

> What is there good or excellent in man
> That is not found in thee? Thy virtues flash;
> They break at once on my astonished soul,
> As if the curtains of the dark were drawn
> To let in day at midnight.

Guilford.   Think me true;
> And though ill-fortune crossed upon our friendship—

Pembroke. Curse on our fortune!—Think!—I know thee honest.

Guilford. For ever I could hear thee—but thy life—
> Oh, Pembroke! linger not—

Pembroke.   And can I leave thee
> Ere I have clasped thee in my. eager arms,
> And giv'n thee back my sad repenting heart?
> Believe me, Guilford, like the Patriarch's dove —
>   (*Embracing*)
> It wandered forth, but found no resting-place
> Till it came forth again to lodge with thee.

The scene does not close, however, until Pembroke flies at the approach of the Lady Jane, whom he dare not face for emotion, and whose coming he compares, in rhymed couplets full of beauties, to the approach of day, when night 'shrinks before the purple-dawning East'.

But though we are glad in that passage to be rid of the 'flowers of eloquence', to force Gray to a pun, their absence deprives the passage of the only sort of poignancy Rowe could give; there is no memorable expression of painful emotion in the whole scene, not one revealing phrase. What Rowe did was to banish admiration from the tragic brew: the pity of unsuccessful, or rather of unfortunate love was there, even though the love was no longer heroic; but the balancing ingredient had gone. There is no driving power in his people, nor in his phrasing: we float along in a vague and not disagreeable flow of words socially recognized as poetic; for if Rowe is the forerunner of Lillo, he is also the distant but indubitable ancestor of Stephen Phillips, and the croonings of *Paolo and Francesca*.

IX

THE MOURNING BRIDE AND CATO

The Mourning Bride, 1697.
Cato, 1713.

IT is not so out of place as it may seem to consider two isolated works of authors who produced no body of tragedy, for both plays were extremely popular in their time, although the reasons which made *Cato* a success were not purely literary; and both are interesting from the critical point of view.

It is not hard to understand why *The Mourning Bride* was hailed as a great work, and why Dryden could write of Congreve:

Heaven that but once was prodigal before,
To Shakespeare gave as much, she could not give him more,

if a stringent course of average Restoration drama has first been undergone. There really is a richness of thought and feeling in Congreve's work which marks it out strongly from all the plays written since *All For Love.* To us it seems an extraordinarily ravelled and unlikely plot. Its gloom is not altogether artificial, but the paraphernalia of the gloom are: in fact, to forestall the expression of three generations later, it is a 'Gothic' play, all chains and dungeons, though the supernatural is wanting. Congreve's object was not didactic, though in his 'Epistle Dedicatory' to the Princess he declared it was; and he is nearer to the mark when he says in the prologue:

To please and move has been our poet's theme,
Art may direct, but nature is his aim;

thus freeing himself from the controversies of the day. It

is true that poetic justice is satisfied, so that the play ends happily; but we feel that pleasure rather than precept urged the event, and if we are cheated of the agreeable sensation of pity which Rowe provides for our delectation, we should feel more cheated if all were not well at the end. We should grumble just as we should if a novel by Mr. Edgar Wallace left us in tears, for, one may as well confess it, *The Mourning Bride* is a thriller rather than a tragedy. Unlike other thrillers, however, it can carry with it a considerable weight of literary, thoughtful, and emotional matter, the slightest intrusion of which into an ordinary novel of excitement and detection at once ruins it.

It is not really a heroic play at all: there is not even the pretence at admiration which persists through to Rowe; love, and love in distress, is certainly the theme, but it is passionate and not heroic love. There is no question of love being the noblest frailty of the mind, nor do we find the introverted, tortured love Otway gives us. There is no heroic valour worth speaking of, and what there is occurs ' off '. It is more like a play of Ford than any other tragedy of the period, though it does not quite come up to that level of consistency. It differs also, not only because it ends happily, but because it never quite gets the dagger under the skin in the way *The Broken Heart* or *'Tis Pity She's a Whore* does. Nevertheless, where it most triumphs is in the expression of passionate feeling, often overwrought. Its success owes practically nothing to structure, nothing at all to ' poetic beauties', for though there is much poetry in the play it is never dragged in without cause. Even the famous opening:

> Music has charms to soothe a savage breast

comes naturally, just as naturally as the opening:

> If music be the food of love, play on,

for, like Shakespeare's, it is part of the expression of the emotion of the moment, and goes on almost at once to :

Almeria. Why am I not at peace ?
Leonora.   Dear Madam, cease,
    Or moderate your griefs ; there is no cause —
Almeria. No cause ! Peace, peace, there is eternal cause,
    And misery eternal will succeed.
    Thou canst not tell—thou hast indeed no cause.

The impact of the phrasing is almost that of nature.

For where Congreve scored heavily over all his contemporaries was in his versification. It may be a bold claim to make, yet it might not be altogether extravagant to make it, that Congreve's blank verse is the best instrument for the drama of his age, better even than Dryden's. It is flexible, flowing and free; it can change its pace and its point of attack upon the nerves; it is full of vowel colour. Congreve knew that there was nothing mystic about verse as such, but that it was simply a useful way of handling words and moulding phrases so that they could be spoken easily from the stage. What he said about operatic recitative in the ' Argument Introductory to the Opera of *Semele* ' may, with allowance for his discussing a different thing, be applied to dramatic verse: it ' is only a more tuneable speaking; it is a kind of prose in music; its beauty consists in coming near nature, and in improving the natural accents of words by more pathetic or emphatical tones '. Thus we rarely feel that his pen has been drilled to perform the movements of the couplet; indeed, often, to think of the couplet when reading *The Mourning Bride*, is to be misled. Take

> Nature. . .
> May lay the burden down, and sink in slumbers
> Of peace eternal.   Death, grim death, will fold
> Me in his leaden arms, and press me close
> To his cold clayey breast ;

where to allow a suspicion of end-stopping on 'fold' is to spoil what is otherwise an excellent rhetorical phrase. Congreve was writing, not blank verse, but dramatic speech; and it is significant of the undramatic mind of the whole of the eighteenth century that Dr. Johnson should have picked out for especial commendation the passage ('How reverent is the face of this tall pile,' etc.: II. iii), which is the most end-stopped in the whole play, and which strikes the modern reader as being the most unreal, the most filled with artificial imagery, of any he can meet with in the course of the tragedy.

Moreover, the lines are internally constructed in a way that neither Lee's nor Otway's nor Rowe's come within sight of being; and here Sir Edmund Gosse ingeniously suggested the influence, if not the deliberate copying, of Milton. Miltonic passages do indeed occur, but they are rare, even if the occasional Miltonic line, such as

> No term, no bound, but infinite of woe

is fairly common, and if here and there an awkward Miltonic inversion crops up. Such passages strike one most where the subject matter is most philosophic, and these passages are the least dramatic both in matter and in movement, for philosophy, to become dramatic, must at least seem to be the immediate outcome of emotion—the thought must occur because passion has driven the brain to thought. We may take a passage:

> O impotence of sight! Mechanic sense,
> Which to exterior objects ow'st thy faculty,
> Not seeing of election, but necessity.
> Thus do our eyes, as do all common mirrors,
> Successively reflect succeeding images;
> Not what they would, but must; a star, or toad,
> Just as the hand of chance administers.
> Not so the mind, whose undetermined view

Revolves, and to the present adds the past :
Essaying further to futurity.   (II. viii.)

But if Congreve had learnt something from Milton of how
to introduce weighty matter into his verse—and Congreve
certainly had a pondering mind, and was fairly well read in
philosophy—his verse really goes back to the best period of
Elizabethan stage blank verse, say to the period between
1600 and 1620: one does not call it Shakespearian, merely
to avoid the possible implications of the word. But take it
on all levels, it is strongly reminiscent of Shakespeare.
First, to look at a piece of humdrum information :

> Our posture of affairs and scanty time,
> My lord, require you should compose yourself,
> And think on what we may reduce to practice.
>
> (III. ii.)

There are scores of passages very similar to that in Shakespeare himself—good, brisk, workmanlike stuff to get over
necessary ground with. The first scene in *Lear* will provide
one; or to take a more impassioned phase :

> I tell thee she's to blame not to have feasted
> When my first foe was laid in earth, such enmity,
> Such detestation bears my blood to his :
> My daughter should have revelled at his death.
> She should have made these palace walls to shake,
> And all the high and ample roof to ring
> With her rejoicings.   What, to mourn, and weep ;
> Then, then to weep, and pray, and grieve ? By Heav'n,
> There's not a slave, a shackled slave of mine,
> But should have smiled that hour, through all his care,
> And shook his chains in transport of rude harmony.
>
> (I. iv.)

Neglecting, perhaps, the use of certain words which might
betray the period, would not anybody hearing that passage
place it rather at the beginning of the century than at the
end ? It is far more free than anything to be found in any

other Restoration dramatist; the movement of the phrasing corresponds much more to the movement of the emotions than, say, Otway's, whose natural diction has come in for praise, and had already in his own day. Where Almeria becomes partly distracted, Congreve very nearly achieved something fine, but spoilt it with 'Gothic' horror overdone, though his passage never nears the ridiculous, as the scene of Belvidera's distraction does. But in his dallyings with horror he does, on one occasion at least, produce a ghastly Tourneurian effect; that is, when Zara, believing she sees the corpse of Osmyn, swallows poison, and lying beside the body, tries to caress the head which has been cut off and taken away to make disguise complete:

> O friendly draught, already in my heart.
> Cold, cold; my veins are icicles and frost.
> I'll creep into his bosom, lay me there;
> Cover us close—or I shall chill his breast,
> And fright him from my arms—See, see, he slides
> Still further from me; look, he hides his face,
> I cannot feel it—quite beyond my reach.
> O now he's gone, and all is dark—   (*Dies.*)   (v. x.)

It is of no use to pretend that this is in the highest ranks of poetry; it is not: but as verse it has enormous virtues which that of his contemporaries lacked. They were not, of course, trying to do the same sort of thing, or if they were they were using different means. Whereas Congreve tried to make the verse take the impress of his thought, they were moulding their thought to take the form and motion of their verse, an eventuality no amount of warning from Dryden could prevent. Where he is at his best is where the feeling is strong enough to carry a certain amount of thought, and there he can make the verse follow the complexities of the mind in a way which has nothing Miltonic about it, but makes us, rather, think of Chapman:

> If piety be thus debarred access
> On high, and of good men the very best
> Is singled out to bleed, and bear the scourge,
> What is reward? or what is punishment?
> But who shall dare to tax eternal justice!
> Yet I may think—I may, I must; for thought
> Precedes the will to think, and error lives
> E'er reason can be born.   Reason, the power
> To guess at right and wrong; the twinkling lamp
> Of wand'ring life, that winks and wakes by turns,
> Fooling the follower, betwixt shade and shining.   (III. i.)

That could not have been done in the polished, balanced verse which was so well able to express Dryden's easy pessimism.

Cato is a very different kettle of fish: it is indeed a kettle into which all the Restoration fish, except one, have been put. That they are puny and undersized, and ought to have been thrown back into the water, does not at the moment matter. There is the military heroism of Portius; the Machiavellism of Sempronius. There are the two brothers in love with the same young woman, one of them concealing his love; there is the unfortunate love of Marcia; there is the noble savage in Juba—Dennis pointed out that the reconciliation scene of Syphax and Juba was a gross parody of that between Antony and Ventidius—there is a reminiscence of youthful prowess in the hunting field; there is the naked breast bared to swords ashamed; and there is, of course, Romanism to any degree. Hardly an author in the genre has not had tribute levied upon him. It might have been a reputable play of its kind had it been written by some one who believed that these ingredients meant something, but Addison evidently did not. The short-faced gentleman who wrote *The Spectator* could hardly be expected to, and that is why the fish are so lamentably small. The mechanical structure will pass in spite of Dennis; but the verse, being stiff and stilted, often unreasonably bad though syllabically correct, conveys neither thought nor feeling. The sense it gives of needing rhyme has already been referred to and illustrated. It is as though the lines had couplet or quatrain structure; and indeed it is surprising how often Addison's speeches run to four lines, or to multiples of four. Even at its freest it is never free, as we may judge from what is, possibly, the best passage of the play:

> The soul, secured in her existence, smiles
> At the drawn dagger, and defies its point.
> The stars shall fade away, the sun himself
> Grow dim with age, and nature sink in years;
> But thou shalt flourish in immortal youth,
> Unhurt amidst the war of elements,
> The wrecks of matter, and the crash of worlds. (v. i.)

Just for a moment the atmosphere of frigidity seems to be slightly thawed: Addison always warmed to the comfortable commonplace; but the verse is still tied to the couplet.

It is, of course, easy enough to destroy *Cato*, and Dennis did so pretty thoroughly in his *Remarks* upon that play, for reasons that are interesting enough as exhibiting the state of theory at that time. They might not all cut much ice with us now, but at least he judged by the event, and not by the doctrine. He claimed that Addison fell into three sorts of absurdities: those due to observing the unities too closely: those due to not observing the unities closely enough; and those which could not be attributed to either cause. Chief among these last is the character of Cato himself, who was framed by Addison to symbolize a new kind of object for admiration—a sage who was also a selfless statesman. It was moral valour, not pragmatic valour, he meant to hold up for praise. But in fact Cato is an intolerable prig, 'who deserted the cause of liberty and of his country, through stubbornness and through ignorance, or sacrificed them to his stoical pride', to borrow from Dennis. He is, indeed, unthinkable. When his son is killed he goes into an ecstasy of joy. Now a man, at all events a man we are expected to admire, may find some consolation in his sorrow to think that his son has died worthily, but he does not want to gloat over the fact and

> view at leisure
> The bloody corse, and count those glorious wounds.

And one wonders that when Juba exclaimed in admiration 'Was ever man like this!' the whole audience did not rise up and shout 'We hope to God not!' To us who have long since accepted the Peace of Utrecht in a philosophic spirit, and who no longer fear Bolingbroke and Nonconformity Bills, the whole thing is little short of nauseating. It is on most counts a thoroughly bad play; but it deserved to be something better.

For Addison was definitely trying, apart from political delicacies, to do something really worth while. He was trying to restore to tragedy an element which had gone out of it, not only with Rowe, but with the rise of the idea of heroic tragedy. He wanted to rid it of sentimentality and to excite our pity, not by unfortunate love—as Dennis noted, the love in *Cato* produces no tragical distress—but by the death of an admirable hero, of a hero whose death meant the destruction of a fine idea. For him the business of tragedy was, as Pope said in the prologue, to show

> A brave man struggling in the storms of fate,
> And greatly falling with a falling state!

There is certainly no miauling in this tragedy, no hawking of broken hearts in exchange for tears. Addison was perfectly on the right lines, and if only he could have made us admire his plaster hero his tragedy might have achieved something.

Again, he had the courage to run counter to the whole stream of Restoration doctrine in his attitude towards poetic justice. Dennis complained that he had ' arraigned and condemned the poetical justice of the stage ', as indeed he had, in *Spectator No. 40*. ' As the principal design of tragedy ', he wrote, ' is to raise commiseration and terror in the minds of the audience, we shall defeat it's great end, if we always make virtue and innocence happy and success-ful.' We should lose all the ' pleasing anguish ' of the tragic emotions. This did not please Dennis, who was bold enough to say that ' 'Tis certainly the duty of every tragic poet, by an exact dispensation of poetical justice, to imitate the divine dispensation, and to inculcate a particular providence '. Not because life is at all so satis-factory, in fact because of the contrary; divine dispensation only working itself out in futurity, which the poet must include in his three hours' traffic of the stage. In this Addison was, of course, perfectly in the right. Dennis was only repeating the old arguments, but Addison saw that if all is well that ends well there can be no tragedy. It is only because the gods are unjust that tragedy exists at all, for if virtue is rewarded and evil punished, terror is at once removed from tragedy. There is no need to labour this point; we can draw an illustration from the popular literature of the present day. One of the reasons why a detective novel is not a tragedy is that we all know from the start that the villain will be caught, and that the really nice people will triumph. But in tragedy, if we take

sides with any one at all, it is with the sufferer. Thus if
Œdipus is, as some say, the first detective story, then it is
a bad one; for though the criminal is discovered, it is
with him, rather than with Creon, that we sympathize. If
tragedy does not make us face what is nearly unbearable,
then it has no reason for existence, and can be of no value
to us in exploring life.

Moreover, Addison had two other virtues. He did not
aim at any kind of prettiness, and is almost devoid of
' flowers of eloquence'; and again, he did not depend upon
any accidental dramatic surprises. This also, in the eyes
of the indefatigable Dennis, is a crime:

> Probability ought certainly to reign in every tragical action,
> but though it ought everywhere to predominate, it ought not
> to exclude the wonderful. . . here there are none of those
> beautiful surprises which are to be found in some of the Grecian
> tragedies, and in some of our own ; and consequently there is
> nothing wonderful, nothing terrible, or deplorable, which all
> three are caused by surprise.

But this, obviously, is to make surprise a little too cheap.
Dennis, who was, up to a point, a sound critic, somewhat
overstepped the bounds of his own theory in this. In fact,
just as the playwrights of these years exhibit the decay of
the heroic form, so Dennis reveals the decay of heroic
criticism : he is not critical enough of his own contradic-
tory ideas, just as Addison did not see the paradox in using
heroic counters for what he was trying to do. The result
is, that though Dennis's attack is devastating enough,
the modern reader is likely after reading it to rally to
Addison's side : for Addison, though so painfully inept in
practice, was in the right where theory was concerned.

The truth is that Addison, in this as in most things of
life, was far too cautious : ' Keep the mid way, the middle
way is best.' If he had frankly abandoned all the precepts

and prabbles of heroic tragedy, and written as his mind dictated, he might have turned out something passable, though he was not enough of a poet to produce anything good. Congreve, on the other hand, by ignoring most of what his contemporary critics were saying, wrote something which has, in places at least, the accents of nature raised to the power of art. Addison also aimed at nature (which is what Dennis, at this stage of his life confusing verisimilitude with realism, reproached him with), but he fell between two stools; and the fact that his fall was softened by an immediate success thanks to political feeling does not make it any the less complete. For in truth the age of heroic tragedy had passed, as surely as constitutional monarchy had come. Fielding and Carey, in writing *Tom Thumb* and *Chrononhotonthologos*, were wasting their time beating a dying dog; though, as Mr. Bateson has pointed out in his admirable *English Comic Drama, 1700–1750*, Carey's work is not so much a criticism, as a fantasy standing on its own legs. Thus the fact remains that *Cato*, while being a return to a better notion of tragedy, by having truck with the heroic ruined its own consistency, and is incontestable proof that the age of the heroic was definitely a bygone thing.

CONCLUSION

It is not by its form, but rather in the choice of material laid upon the form, that Restoration tragedy is condemned to a secondary place. The error arose through limiting the elements in human nature which were supposed fit for the purposes of art. This is always fatal, for no one, if not the artist, can say that nothing human is outside his interests. The fault is not, of course, in selection itself; the error lies further back in the processes of art, and is often to be traced in work professedly didactic. It is not only that, in Keats's phrase, we hate a poem that has a palpable design upon us; nor is it that art can be cut off from its ethical background—at least not easily; but it is emphatically that no art can be really great which does not accept humanity for what it is. The moment it tries to guide mankind into channels, or endeavours to prevent its being mankind, an essential element is omitted. For this reason we find, in our own day, something lacking in the work of Mr. Shaw and Mr. Wells which is present in that of Hardy and Mr. Kipling.

It is agreed that the virtues of the classical method are selection and an austere exclusion of all that is not to the point; but unless the right things are left in, so that their relationship mirrors the general relationship of things in the more doubtful arena of daily life, the right balance is not struck. The classical form enhances not only the good, when good there is, but also the evil when it is there; also, where the art itself is concerned, it brings out whatever may be good, but it makes the bad even worse. And in Restoration tragedy, instead of the content creating a form proper to it, romantic, that is to say immature, undisciplined passions were made to flow into a classical mould, with the consequent sense of discomfort we experience in many of these plays. One or two are superbly successful; here and there we find some adequate ones; but there is no large body of good work simply because the form does not correspond with the emotion. Perhaps the drama was not the right form at all for the emotion which was to be symbolized; there was, as we have seen, a confusion between tragedy and the epic, and it may be no mere accident that the pre-eminent work of the period should be *Paradise Lost*.

Moreover, if admiration, by an exclusion which led to distortion, was one of the causes of the failure of this tragedy to maintain its place, its treatment of love contributed another cause. Love, because it is in the nature of things a private emotion, a man's attitude towards it varied and biased by all manner of accidents, is weak as a main element in tragedy. Aristophanes was right to deplore its introduction by Euripides. For tragic terror and pity are elemental emotions; confuse them, and the balance is lost. In the prologue to *Cato* Pope very aptly remarked:

In pitying love we but our weakness show,

and Dryden himself, in his preface to *All for Love*, put his finger upon the source of the trouble: 'That which is wanting to work up the pity to a greater height', he said, ' was not afforded me by the story: for the crimes of love which they both committed were not occasioned by any necessity, or fatal ignorance, but were wholly voluntary, since our passions are, or ought to be [delightful alternative!] within our power.' For in tragedy it is the spectacle of man pitting himself against the inevitable which is moving; and since love was the main element relied upon to produce pity, the structure of tragedy was threatened at its base. Finally, it was an art of escape, not of profound realization; that is, it explored the chimerical rather than the actual.

At the same time, though the tragedy of the period is of minor importance, it does occupy a high place, higher than that to be claimed by any drama that has succeeded it, with the exception of Ibsen's and Strindberg's. If, in expelling psychological subtlety, it reduced character too much to a cipher, at least it gave plot the foremost place (except where pretty verbiage got a stranglehold), a place which it yields to character to the detriment of the drama; for character is only the secondary symbol, meant to give life to the poet's main symbol, which is the plot. And whatever the defects it gave birth to, the dramatic theory and practice of that day did at least make a distinction between art and life. It ignored the hint given it by Elizabethan domestic drama; but once George Lillo, by his *London Merchant* (1730), inveigled men into believing that tragedy might be made out of humdrum events within the reach of everybody's knowledge or personal experience, European drama entered upon that descent into naturalism from which even the Scandinavian example does not seem to have been able to rescue it, although in this respect the signs are hopeful. The complaint often heard that modern drama is too 'literary' is a reaction against this, but the analysis is false. The disease from which modern drama is suffering is not literature, but literalness: it is not literary enough; that is, it does not imply tradition, the accumulated experience of humanity. Literature becomes 'literary' in the bad sense only when it ceases to embody the attitudes and emotions of its readers or hearers, when it is separated from life not by being richer, but by being poorer than what we know. Thus *Cato* is 'literary' in this sense, while *Aureng-Zebe* is not, or at least was not. Much of the later Shakespearian tragedy, Massinger's for instance, is also literary in a way that *Tamburlaine* was not. When a school or movement decays it rings hollow not because the forms it produces are bad, but because they are not properly filled. This is what happened to Restoration tragedy.

Nor, certainly, has it been lucky in its descendant, namely, popular melodrama, which contains all the elements of the 'noble' and the 'heroic', and the pity for unfortunate love. *The Only Way* and the boulevard successes of M. Henri Bernstein are the progeny, after several generations, of *Sophonisba* and *The Conquest of Granada*. For as far as writing is concerned, you can always pour new wine into old bottles; but if you continually pour old wine into any bottles at all it grows musty. This is exactly what has happened with this drama. But it is well to be able to distinguish between the vintage in its prime and when it has reached the stage of being undrinkable.

A BRIEF BIBLIOGRAPHY

The following lists are not intended to be complete. They consist of books which I have from time to time found useful, and they cover the ground fairly completely.

LIST OF PLAYS

First editions of collected works are given, and the first editions of *The Mourning Bride* and *Cato*. A few more recent or standard editions are added, as well as those editions, marked with an asterisk, which have been used for quotation in the text ; not because they were superior, but because they were to hand.

Dryden, John.

    1701. Tonson Ed. 2 vols.

    1717. Congreve's Ed. 6 vols.

    *1762. Tonson Ed. with Congreve's Introduction. 6 vols.

    *1808. Scott. 18 vols.

    1882–1893. Scott—Saintsbury Ed. 18 vols.

    1904. Mermaid Ed. Introduction by G. Saintsbury. 2 vols.

    1932. Nonesuch Ed. by Montague Summers. 6 vols.

Lee, Nathaniel.

    1713. Wellington. 2 vols.

    *1734. Printed for Feales and others. 3 vols.

Otway, Thomas.

    1712. Tonson. 2 vols.

    *1757. Printed for Hitch and others. 3 vols.

    1813. Edition by T. Thornton.   [1 vol.

    1891 and 1903. Mermaid Ed. Introduction by R. Noel.

    1926. Nonesuch Ed. by Montague Summers. 3 vols.

    1932. Edition by J. C. Ghosh. Oxford. 2 vols.

Rowe, Nicholas.

    1720. Tawney. 2 vols.

    1727. London. 3 vols.

    1736. London. 2 vols.   [others. 2 vols.

    *1747. Anne Devenish Ed. Printed for Lintot, Tonson and

    1929. *Three Plays*, ed. J. R. Sutherland.

Congreve, William.

    1697. *The Mourning Bride.*

    1710. Works. 3 vols.

Congreve, William (*continued*):

    1887. Mermaid Ed. Introduction by A. C. Ewald. 1 vol.

    1923. Nonesuch Ed. by Montague Summers. 4 vols.

    *1928. *The Mourning Bride*. World's Classics. *Congreve Vol. II*.
Addison, Joseph.

    1713. *Cato*.

    1721. Ed. Tickell. 4 vols.

    1854. Bohn's Ed. 6 vols.

    *1928. *Cato* in World's Classics. *Five Restoration Tragedies*.†

Banks and Settle do not exist in collected editions. I have quoted from old copies. Crowne was edited in 1873 by Maidment and Logan, 4 vols. (*Dramatists of the Restoration*. 1872, &c.)

Note. In transcribing passages from the plays, I have modernized the spelling and capitalization; and, where the scansion would permit, the apostrophes. I have also, very rarely, tampered with the punctuation. For Chapter IV, I have relied on the Oxford Shakespeare; and Grosart's edition of Daniel, Spenser Society, 1885, 4 vols.

GENERAL HISTORY OF THE PERIOD

Aubrey. *Brief Lives*. Clark. Oxford University Press. 1898.

Burnet, Bishop G. *History of His Own Time*.   [2 vols.

Clark, G. N. *The Later Stuarts, 1660-1714*. Oxford. 1934.

Evelyn. *Diary*.

Gooch, G. P. *Political Thought from Bacon to Halifax*. Home University Library.

Hamilton. *Memoirs of Grammont*.

Macaulay, Lord. *History of England*.

Pepys. *Diary*.

Spence. *Anecdotes*.

Of those books well known and often reprinted, I have not given details of editions.

STAGE HISTORY

Baker, D. E. *Biographica Dramatica*. 1782.

Cibber, Colley. *Apology*. 1740.

† That volume contains *All for Love*; *Venice Preserv'd*; *Oroonoko*; *The Fair Penitent*, and *Cato*.

The World's Classics volume, *Five Heroic Plays*, contains Orrery's *Mustapha*; Crowne's *Destruction of Jerusalem* (Part II); Lee's *Sophonisba*; Dryden's *Aureng-Zebe*; and Settle's *Empress of Morocco*.

Cibber, Theophilus (and Shiels). *Lives of the Poets.* 1753.

Downes. *Roscius Anglicanus.* 1708.

Genest. *Some Account of the English Stage, 1660–1830.* Bath, 1832. 10 vols.

Langbaine. *English Dramatic Poets.* 1691.
Gildon's continuation, 1699.

Nicoll, Allardyce. *British Drama.* 1925.
The Development of the Theatre. 1927.

Oldys. *Biographia Britannica.* (Articles in) 1747–1760.

CRITICAL

The only books known to me which deal solely with this type of play are:

Beljame, A. *Le Public et les Hommes de Lettres en Angleterre, 1660–1744,* 1881: trs. E. O. Lorimer as *Men of Letters and the English Public in the Eighteenth Century.* 1948.

Chase, H. N. *The English Heroic Play.* Columbia University Press. 1903.

Works on the period are:

Charlanne. *L'Influence Française en Angleterre au XVIIᵉᵐᵉ Siècle.* Paris. 1906.

Elwin, Malcolm. *The Playgoers' Handbook to the Restoration Drama.* Cape. 1928.

Krutch, J. W. *Comedy and Conscience after the Restoration.* Columbia University Press, N.Y. 1924. [1922.

Nicoll, Allardyce. *Dryden as an Adapter of Shakespeare.* Milford.
Restoration Drama, 1660–1700. Cambridge University Press. 1923.
XVIII Century Drama, 1700–1750. Cambridge University Press. 1925.

Taine. *History of English Literature.*

Ward, A. W. *English Dramatic Literature* (to the Death of Queen Anne). Macmillan, revised edition 1899. 3 vols.

Cambridge History of English Literature, vol. viii.

Contemporary critical opinions may be found in:

Addison, Joseph, *Tatlers* and *Spectators, passim.*

Collier, Jeremy. *A Short View of the Profaneness and Immorality of the Stage.* 1698.

Corneille, Pierre. *Trois Discours,* and the *Avis, Préfaces,* and *Défenses* of his plays.

Dennis, John. *The Usefulness of the Stage.* 1698.
Remarks on Cato. 1713.

Dryden, John. Dedications of and prefaces to his plays, especially *An Essay of Dramatic Poesy*, 1668; and Ker, W. P., *Essays of John Dryden*, Clarendon Press, 1900. 2 vols.

Langbaine. *English Dramatic Poets*, 1691. Gildon's continuation, 1699.

Pope, Alexander *Epistle to Augustus*. 1733.

Racine, Jean. *Prefaces* to plays.

Steele, Richard. *Tatlers, Spectators, The Theatre, passim.*

Critical Essays of the Seventeenth Century, edited by Spingarn, J. E., Clarendon Press, 1908, 3 vols., is the most useful of books on the subject, containing selections from the most important writers of the period (excepting Dryden), and an admirable *Introduction.*

BIOGRAPHICAL: or Specialized Criticism, besides the Works already quoted

General. *The Dictionary of National Biography.*

Dr. Johnson, *Lives of the Poets* (except for Lee).

Dryden. Eliot, T. S. *Homage to John Dryden.* Hogarth Press, 1924.

Lubbock, A. *The Character of John Dryden.* Hogarth Press, 1925.

Nichol Smith, D. *John Dryden*, 1950 (The Clark Lectures).

Saintsbury, G. *John Dryden.* 1881. English Men of Letters.

Scott, Sir W. *Life.* Saintsbury's edition.

Van Doren, M. *The Poetry of John Dryden.* N.Y. 1920.

Verrall, A. W. *Lectures on Dryden.* Cambridge University Press. 1914.

Congreve. Gosse, Sir E. *Life of William Congreve.* 1888.

Protopopesco, Dr. G. *Congreve, Sa Vie, Son Œuvre.* La Vie Universitaire, 1924.

Addison. Aikin, Lucy. *Life of Joseph Addison.* 1843.

Courthope, W. J. *Addison.* English Men of Letters. 1884.

Dobrée, B. *Essays in Biography.* 1925.

Macaulay, Lord. Review of Aikin's *Life.* 1843. *Collected Essays.*

Smithers, P. *The Life of Joseph Addison.* 1954.

I have found nothing of the lives of Otway, Lee, and Rowe, except in books under other headings in the Bibliography.

INDEX

PRINTED IN GREAT BRITAIN
AT THE UNIVERSITY PRESS, OXFORD
BY VIVIAN RIDLER
PRINTER TO THE UNIVERSITY